Unlocking Hangul – Learning Korean Alphabet

All-in-One Textbook to Learn Korean Language from Zero with Fluent Pronunciation Practice & Writing Hangul Workbook for Beginners

Written by	Korean Study Cafe
Edited by	배혜수 Hye Su Bae
Proofread by	크리스 영진 정 Chris YJ Chung
Designed & Illustrated by	배혜수 Hye Su Bae, 배성현 Sung-hyeon Bae
Audio & Visual content by	배혜수 Hye Su Bae
Published by	Korean Study Cafe
Website	koreanstudycafe.com
E-mail	hello@koreanstudycafe.com

Copyright © 2023 Korean Study Café All rights reserved

No part of this book may be reproduced or transmitted in any form or by any means, electronic or mechanical, including photocopying, recording, or by any information storage and retrieval system, without written permission from the publisher.

이 책의 내용을 사전 서면 허가 없이 전재하거나 복제할 경우 법적인 제재를 받게 됨을 알려 드립니다.

How to use this book

General

The general notation of this book is referred to and presented based on the standard Korean dictionary of the National Institute of Korean Language (korean.go.kr). However, this book adopts the word "Hangul" instead of "Hangeul" as it's more commonly known to English speakers, although NIKL states "Hangeul" is the correct spelling. Also, a few exceptional contents are mentioned in the book.

Pronunciation

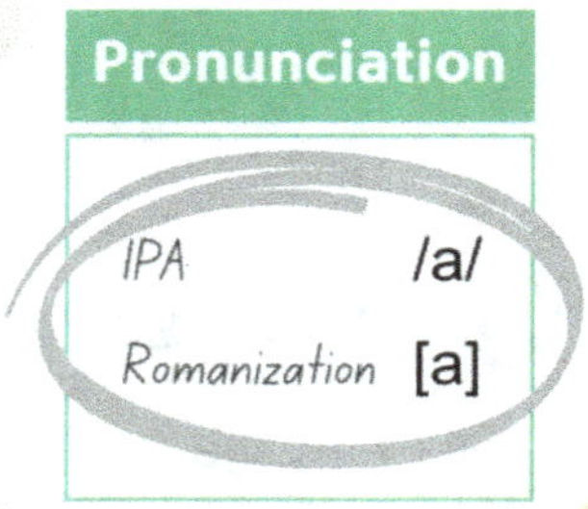

Pronunciations are described according to the IPA(International Phonetic Alphabet) guide and romanizations, which are indicated with slashes(/ /) for IPA and with square brackets([ ]) for romanizations describing the closest sound of each letter.

Writing practice

The book engages learners to practice tracing letters with the grey-colored guides first and gives readers the opportunity to practice writing them.

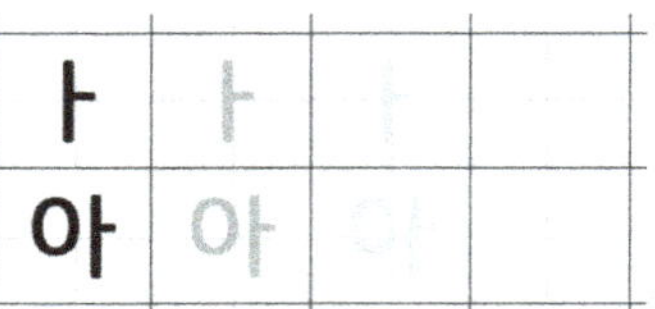

You can ask us any questions!

You can email us via **"hello@koreanstudycafe.com"** or leave a comment on video or audio materials if you have a question about the content. We will happily respond to any inquiries.

Access to extra materials

(Audio, Video & Flashcard)

The password-protected webpage is ONLY available for book purchasers. You can access audio files, video lessons, online flashcards, etc. It does NOT require any of your personal information or further action. Simple and Easy!

QR CODE to go to the page directly

Page address: koreanstudycafe.com/book/unlocking-hangul-bonus/
Password: sejong (Password to access any restricted content in this book)

Audio material

This exposes you to native speakers' frequently used pronunciation. We provide you with (1) a Youtube Podcast version and (2) a Downloadable MP3 version. Both contain the same content. You can play it according to the track number guide in the book.

Video lesson

You can watch video lessons about single vowels to compound batchims via exclusive YouTube links only for the book readers on the page provided above. Also, you can leave a question in the comment section and get the answer directly from us.

Flashcard

The online flashcards are available on the web page mentioned above. It will help you memorize the pronunciations and letters of Hangul.

Korean Study Cafe

The Korean Study Café was established to support Korean language enthusiasts globally. We are immensely proud to offer a variety of free educational resources, including podcasts, Instagram posts, blog articles, and more. In addition to free educational resources, we offer personalized individual and group classes that have been instrumental in aiding hundreds of students to improve their Korean language proficiency; not only fosters personal growth but also catapults them forward in their respective careers, armed with a deepened understanding and proficiency in the Korean language.

We aspire to assist all Korean language enthusiasts, but our time and resources are finite, making it challenging to guide everyone personally. We have conducted extensive research and invested in various Hangul textbooks available in the market to suggest appropriate books for self-learners. However, finding a book that comprehensively and clearly explains Hangul, particularly regarding pronunciation intricacies, has proven to be a significant challenge.

To bridge this gap, we have dedicated months to polishing materials to create a comprehensive guide for readers of varying ages, from teens to adults, who are keen on learning Korean.

Our goal is to provide a comprehensive understanding of Hangul as a dynamic writing system characterized by principles and patterns that shape the Korean language. We have crafted detailed sections that explain the intricacies of pronunciation modifications and phenomena, guiding readers to pronounce Korean similarly to native speakers.

Embarking on a journey through this book will be akin to stepping through the first gateway to fully grasp the richness of the Korean language and its intertwined culture. As your trusty guide on this educational voyage, we invite readers to unlock the doors to Hangul with us.

Join us in this enriching journey, and let's unlock the world of Hangul together!

 ## Where to find Korean Study Cafe online content

Instagram   instagram.com/koreanstudycafe.official

Podcast   Korean Study Cafe / Available on Spotify or iTunes

X(Twitter)   twitter.com/KoreanStudyCafe

Facebook   facebook.com/koreanstudycafe

Email   hello@koreanstudycafe.com

Website   koreanstudycafe.com

* If you have any questions or concerns, reach us at : email & website

Table of Contents

 koreanstudycafe.official

koreanstudycafe.official
드디어 한국 여행 시작!
My journey in Korea has finally begun.

CHAPTER 1

Concept of Hangul
한글의 개념

Overview of Hangul

Hangul(한글), the Korean writing system, also known as the Korean alphabet, was created by King Sejong the Great in 1443 with the aim of making it easier for the common people to learn and write. It is currently the official script in South and North Korea(It is called 'Joseongeul' in the North) and is used by Korean descendants globally.

Korean vowel *Pronunciation: /IPA/*

In Korean, there are eight(8) single vowels 단모음 and thirteen(13) compound vowels 이중 모음, in a total of twenty-one(21) letters.

SINGLE VOWEL

Vowel	ㅏ	ㅓ	ㅗ	ㅜ	ㅡ	ㅣ	ㅐ	ㅔ
Pronunciation	/a/	/ʌ/ /ə/	/o/	/u/ /ʊ/	/ɯ/	/i/ /iː/	/ɛ/	/æ/ /e/

COMPOUND VOWEL

Based on 'ㅣ'	Vowel	ㅑ	ㅕ	ㅛ	ㅠ	ㅒ	ㅖ	
	Pronunciation	/ja/	/jʌ/	/jo/	/ju/	/jɛ/	/je/	
Based on 'ㅗ, ㅜ, ㅡ'	Vowel	ㅘ	ㅚ**	ㅙ	ㅞ	ㅝ	ㅟ**	ㅢ
	Pronunciation	/wa/	/we/	/wɛ/	/we/	/wʌ/	/wi/	/ɨi/

** The vowels 'ㅚ' and 'ㅟ' were originally created and pronounced as single vowels in the past. However, nowadays, the pronunciations have evolved efficiently and are produced as compound vowels. (To know more about this, go to page 20)

Korean Consonant   *Pronunciation: /IPA/*

There are fourteen(14) single consonants 단자음 and five(5) double consonants 쌍자음, in a total of nineteen(19) consonants in Korean. The consonants can be categorized into two different classifications. One is by the way it is written, and another is by the sound.

- **Written classification**
  - Single and double consonants depend on the number of component consonants.

SINGLE CONSONANT

Consonant	ㄱ	ㄴ	ㄷ	ㄹ	ㅁ	ㅂ	ㅅ
Name	기역 [gi-yeok]	니은 [ni-eun]	디귿 [di-geut]	리을 [ri-eul]	미음 [mi-eum]	비읍 [bi-eup]	시옷 [si-ot]
Pronunciation	/g/ /k/	/n/	/d/ /t/	/r/ /l/	/m/	/b/ /p/	/s/

Consonant	ㅇ	ㅈ	ㅊ	ㅋ	ㅌ	ㅍ	ㅎ
Name	이응 [i-eung]	지읒 [ji-eut]	치읓 [chi-eut]	키읔 [ki-euk]	티읕 [ti-eut]	피읖 [pi-eup]	히읗 [hi-eut]
Pronunciation	silent	/tʃ/	/tʃʰ/	/kʰ/	/tʰ/	/pʰ/	/h/

DOUBLE CONSONANT

Consonant	ㄲ	ㄸ	ㅃ	ㅆ	ㅉ
Name	쌍기역 [ssang-gi-yeok]	쌍디귿 [ssang-di-geut]	쌍비읍 [ssang-bi-eup]	쌍시옷 [ssang-si-ot]	쌍지읒 [ssang-ji-eut]
Pronunciation	/k'/	/t'/	/p'/	/s'/	/tʃ'/

- **Sound classification**
  - Flat consonants are the base sounds. (Refer to page 35, 104)
  - Aspirated consonants are with wind pressure. (Refer to page 35, 104)
  - Tense consonants are with strained vocal sounds. (Refer to page 104)

Flat	ㄱ /g/ /k/	ㄷ /d/ /t/	ㅂ /b/ /p/	ㅅ /s/	ㅈ /tʃ/
Aspirated	ㅋ /kʰ/	ㅌ /tʰ/	ㅍ /pʰ/	–	ㅊ /tʃʰ/
Tense	ㄲ /k'/	ㄸ /t'/	ㅃ /p'/	ㅆ /s'/	ㅉ /tʃ'/

The letters of Hangul were created **by using the shapes of vocal organs and elements that were believed to comprise the universe,** which were sky, land, and human. Hangul is a phonogram representing almost all sounds and was developed using hieroglyphic (pictorial) principles.

The principle of creating Korean vowels

The basic vowels in Hangul, also known as single vowels, were created using three components: a dot representing the sky (·), a horizontal line representing the land (一), and a vertical line representing a standing human body (|). Compound vowels were created by adding strokes or combining them with other vowels.

The principle of creating Korean consonants

The Korean consonants were created based on the shapes of our vocal organs, such as lips, teeth, gum, throat, and tongue.

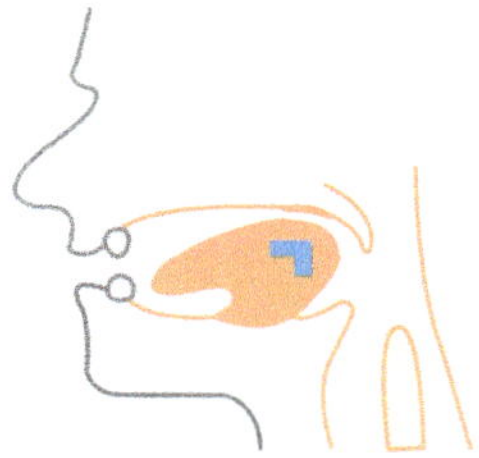

ㄱ It's created to reflect the movement of our tongue blocking the half space between the roof of our mouth and our throat.

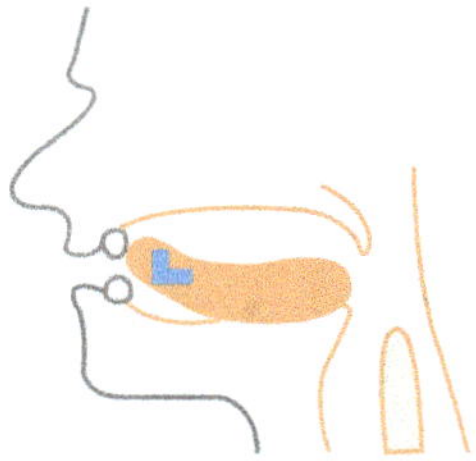

ㄴ It's created to reflect the movement of our tongue touching our upper gum.

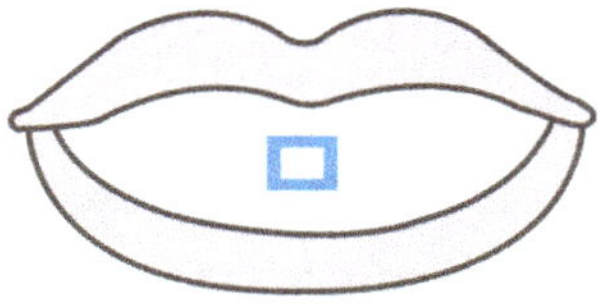

ㅁ It's created to reflect the shape of our lips when producing its sound.

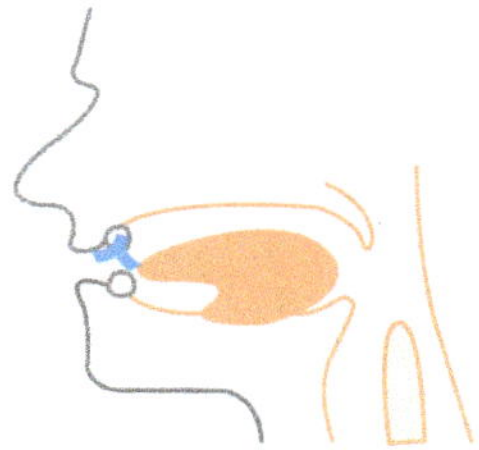

ㅅ It's created to reflect the shape that represents our upper teeth and tongue almost touching each other.

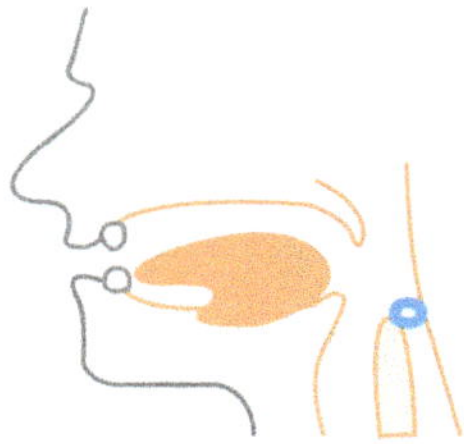

ㅇ It's created to reflect the shape of the air movement in our throat when producing its sound.

Related sounding consonants were created by adding a stroke or the same consonant.

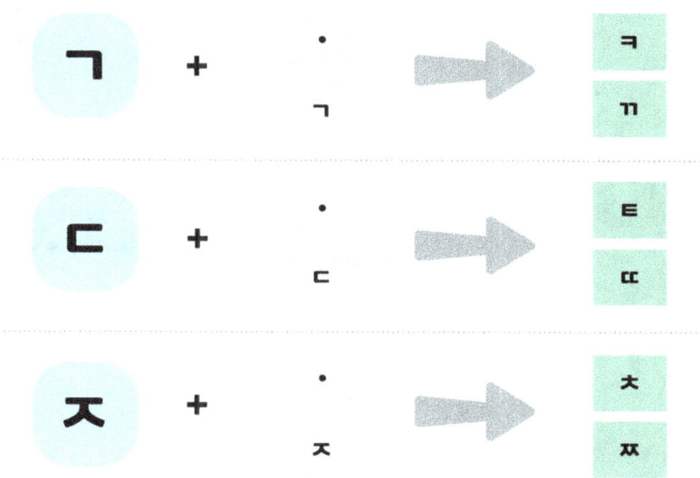

Korean Syllable Block

A distinctive aspect of the Korean language is that a syllable cannot consist of just one vowel or consonant. In Korean, **a syllable must be a combination of at least one consonant and one vowel**, and it can also have additional consonants known as Batchim(받침). It is crucial to maintain the square shape of a syllable.

1 The foundation form of a syllable

This category includes two different forms that depend on the shape of the vowel. If the vowel is vertically long, the consonant should be placed on the left of the vowel. Conversely, if the vowel is horizontally long, the consonant should be placed above the vowel.

Vertically long-shaped vowels?

C V

Their base is "ㅣ" which is vertically long shaped. This group includes: ㅏ, ㅓ, ㅣ, ㅐ, ㅔ, ㅕ, ㅕ, ㅒ, ㅖ

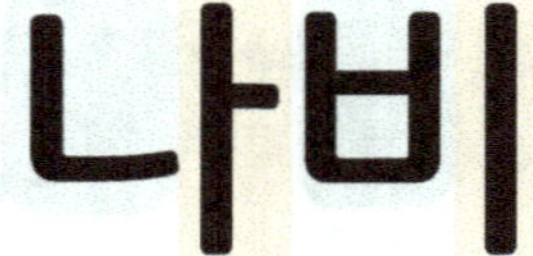

Butterfly
[nabi]

C: Consonant

V: Vowel

Horizontally long-shaped vowels?

C
V

Their base is "ㅡ" which is horizontally long shaped. This group includes: ㅗ, ㅜ, ㅡ, ㅛ, ㅠ

Lake
[hosu]

② The foundation form + <u>ONE Batchim</u>

The syllable blocks in this category are formed by adding ONE BATCHIM, also known as a "final consonant" or "consonant base" to the foundation form on the left page. The correct order for writing and reading a syllable is foundation form first (Consonant to Vowel), then the Batchim. (To see the details about Batchim, refer to page 120)

With a vertically long vowel | **With a horizontally long vowel**

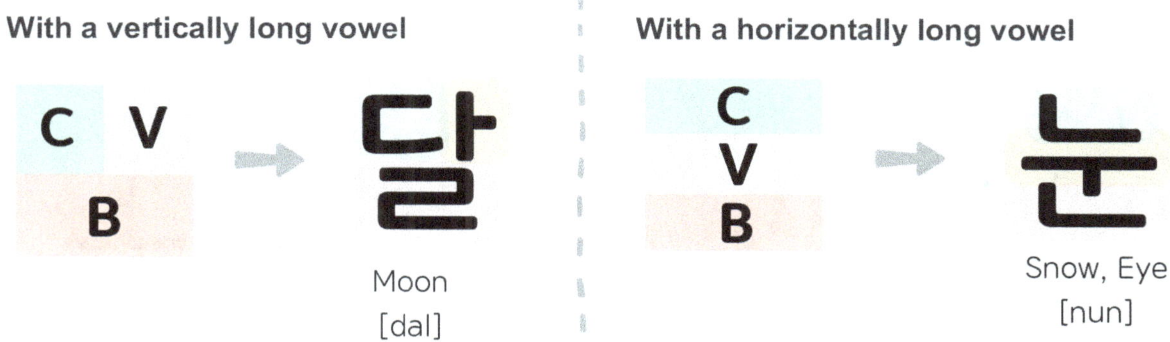

Moon
[dal]

Snow, Eye
[nun]

③ The foundation form + <u>TWO Batchims</u> (Double or Compound one)

This type is created with TWO batchims, which can be double batchim(two same letters) or compound batchim(two different letters). When you read the syllable having this one, pronounce it with one of two batchims according to the rule. (To see the details, refer to page 142)

With a vertically long vowel
(This example is with <u>a double batchim</u>)

With a horizontally long vowel
(This example is with <u>a compound batchim</u>)

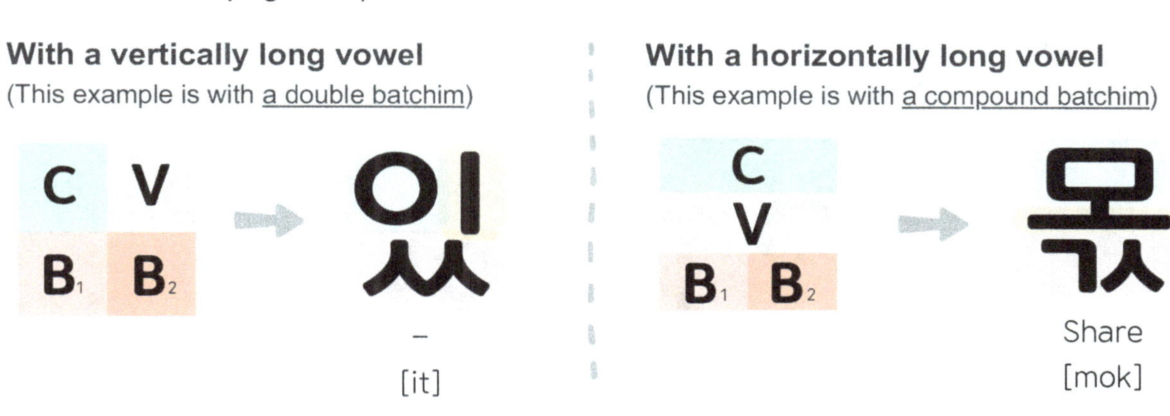

–
[it]

Share
[mok]

C: Consonant
V: Vowel
B: Batchim

Why can't one letter stand alone?

The vowel's position is crucial to maintain the square shape of each syllable block. Suppose the vowel is in the wrong position. In that case, the syllable block's square shape is disrupted and becomes unreadable. Therefore, if only a vowel sound is needed, it can be paired with the silent consonant 'ㅇ(이응).' Conversely, if only a consonant sound is needed, it can be paired with the vowel 'ㅡ[으]' in most cases.

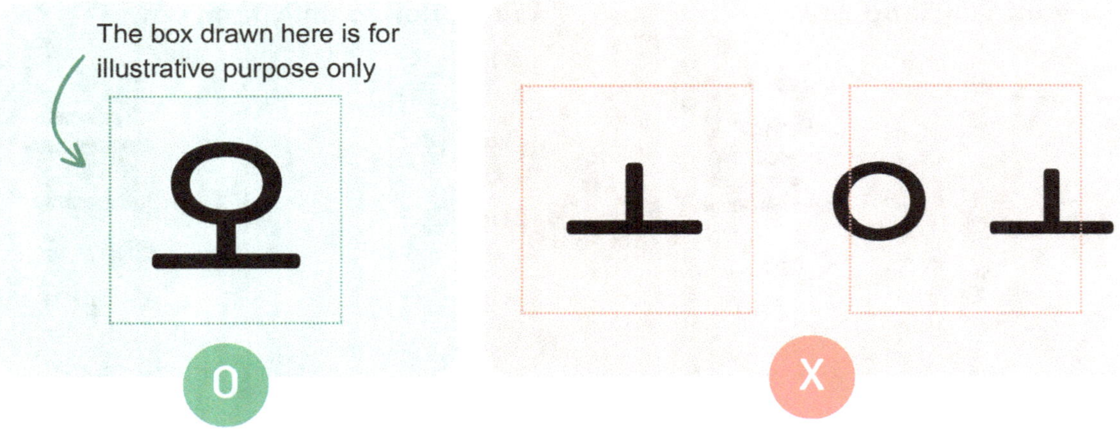

How to keep block shape with compound vowel?

To correctly form a syllable with a compound vowel, imagine breaking it down into its constituent parts and placing each part in its designated spot. For example, the compound vowel "ㅘ" is composed of "ㅗ" and "ㅏ". So, "ㅗ" should be placed underneath the consonant, and "ㅏ" should be placed to the right of the consonant, resulting in the syllable "와". Although the vowel can be disassembled, it's important to note that compound vowels are considered one vowel, not two separate vowels. (To know about compound vowels, see page 68)

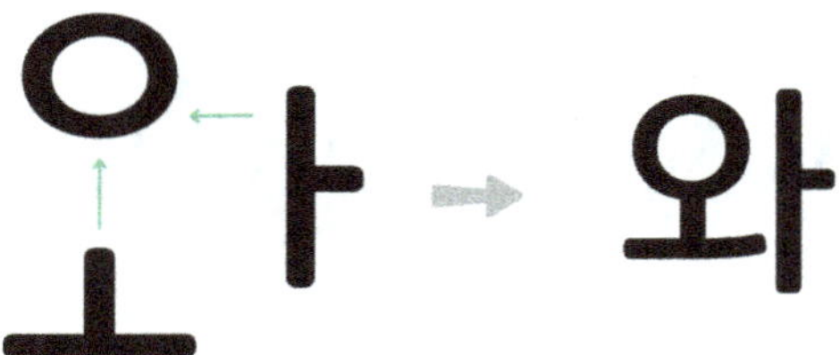

How to Write Korean Letters Properly

Yes, there is, and we recommend you follow it. All Koreans are taught to write Hangul using a specific stroke order in their education. However, each individual may have their own unique writing style because it is no strict rule. Nonetheless, most Korean teachers recommend following the stroke order because it can make writing easier and more efficient. Using proper stroke order can improve your handwriting quality and reduce any miscommunication.

Writing Korean letters

The stroke order always starts **"from left to right"** and **"from top to bottom"**. For example,

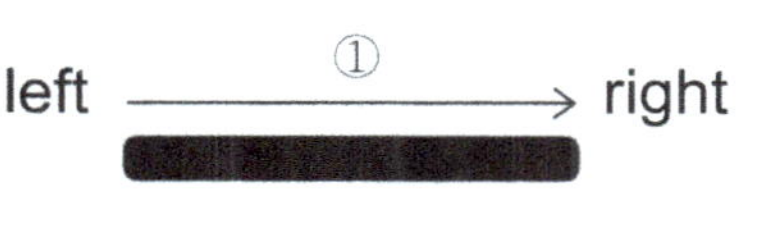

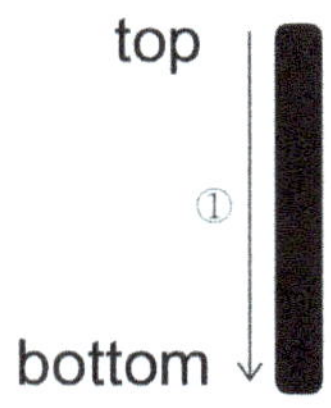

Let's practice!

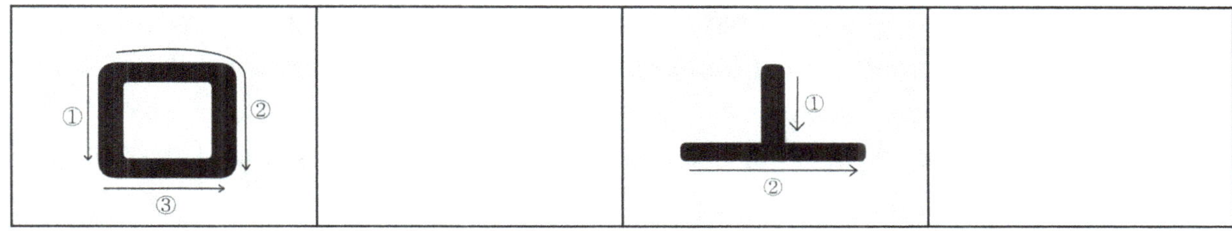

10 key on Korean Keyboard
천지인[Chun-ji-in] 키보드
Sky, Land, Human

Today, most Koreans prefer using the 표준 (Standard) keyboard style for their smartphones. However, there are still some who prefer the older 천지인 (10-key) button keyboard that was popular during the 2G phone era. It's worth noting that using the 10-key keyboard requires a good grasp of the fundamental principles of Hangul since it's not arranged alphabetically like other 10-number key styles used in other countries.

 The principle of 10 key (천지인)

The 천지인 (10 key) keyboard follows the same principle as 한글 (Hangul) creation, with 천 (sky), 지 (land), and 인 (human). Understanding this principle makes it easier to use, as the limited ten keys make it less likely to make typing errors compared to a standard keyboard with 26 keys.

First, the keyboard's top row consists of three buttons (ㅣ, ·, ㅡ) which are used to create any Korean vowel. (To see the principle again, see page 10). Essentially, 'ㅣ' is used as a base for vertically long-shaped vowels, '·' for small strokes, and 'ㅡ' as a base for horizontally long-shaped vowels. For instance, to type the vowel 'ㅚ', press buttons 2-3-1 in that order. Simple! Right?

Typing consonants is even simpler. As we already know, there are close relationships among similar-looking consonants like 'ㄱ', 'ㅋ', and 'ㄲ'. To type one of these, tap button 1. Press it once for 'ㄱ', twice for 'ㅋ', and thrice for 'ㄲ'. So to type the syllable '코끼리', press buttons 코(4-4-2-3) 끼(4-4-4-1) 리(5-5-1) in that order.

What is the button  (or ⌣) for in this keyboard?

Sometimes you need to type two different consonants using one button in a row. For example, when you try to type '부엌과', pressing the number 4 key multiple times to type ㄱ after ㅋ doesn't properly type it. Here is where you tap the arrow button( or ⌣) after typing ㅋ, and you can write ㄱ again without interruption.

Let's practice!

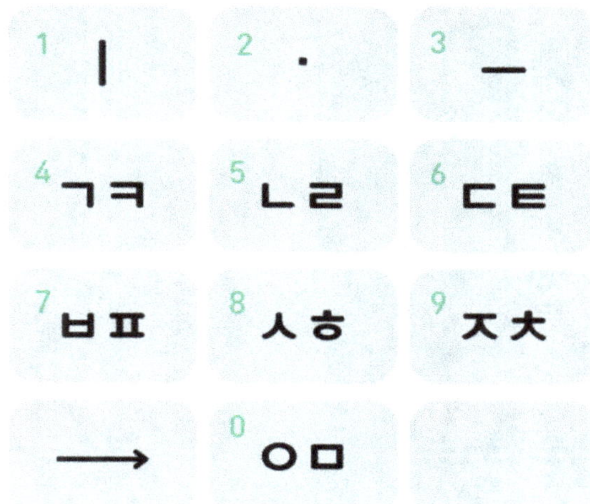

(보기) 한국어 88125 4324 021	1) 받침
2) 김치	3) 떡볶이
4) 세종대왕	5) 사랑해요

 **(1)** 받침 7126 99100 **(2)** 김치 4100 991 **(3)** 떡볶이 666214 723444 01 **(4)** 세종대왕 8211 9230 6121 023120 **(5)** 사랑해요 812 55120 88121 0223

koreanstudycafe.official

koreanstudycafe.official
오늘 한복을 입고 경복궁 구경을 했다. 한복 진짜 예쁘다.
Today I tried on Hanbok and had a tour of Gyeongbokgung Palace. Hanbok is so pretty.

SEOUL
ADMITTED
JUL 16

CHAPTER 2

Learn Hangul

한글을 배워요

1. Single Vowel

단모음

The vowel is the sound made without interruption in our vocal organs, such as 'a, e, i, o, u' in English. In Korean, there are eight(8) single vowels, where your mouth shape at first and at last are the same when making the sound.

Korean single vowels *Pronunciation: /IPA/*

Vowel	ㅏ	ㅓ	ㅗ	ㅜ	ㅡ	ㅣ	ㅐ*	ㅔ*
Pronun-ciation	/a/	/ʌ/ /ə/	/o/	/u/ /ʊ/	/ɯ/	/i/ /iː/	/ɛ/	/æ/ /e/
Name	아	어	오	우	으	이	애	에

* The vowels "ㅐ" and "ㅔ" are pronounced almost the same in daily conversation. (To learn more, refer to pages 28-29)

A debate regarding single vowels in Korean

The National Institute of Korean Language (hereinafter referred to as "NIKL") prescribes that Korean single vowels are ten(10) like the ones on the next page. That's because ten(10) vowels including 'ㅚ' and 'ㅟ' were originally created as single vowels. However, over time, the two vowels sound 'ㅚ' and 'ㅟ' were optimized and evolved efficiently, gradually pronounced as compound vowels.

For that reason, there is controversy over categorizing 'ㅚ' and 'ㅟ' as single or compound vowels. Despite the controversy, the NIKL officially states that there are ten(10) single vowels in Korean following the original classification system. However, they also state that these two vowels can be considered compound vowels.

Therefore, through this book, we will be referring to eight(8) single vowels following the general understanding and concept of Korean letters and pronunciation that can be applied in everyday conversation instead of adhering to theoretical rules.

To know about compound vowels, see page 68

Original Korean single vowels (This is what NIKL categorizes them)	Total of ten (10) ㅏ, ㅓ, ㅗ, ㅜ, ㅡ, ㅣ, ㅐ, ㅔ, ㅚ, ㅟ
Modern Korean single vowels (This is what Koreans consider in everyday conversation)	Total of eight (8) ㅏ, ㅓ, ㅗ, ㅜ, ㅡ, ㅣ, ㅐ, ㅔ

How to distinguish 'ㅐ' and 'ㅔ'?

When Hangul was first created, the vowels 'ㅐ' and 'ㅔ' were pronounced differently. The key difference between the two is the shape of the mouth when pronouncing. The size of the mouth opening is larger when pronouncing 'ㅐ', while the size is smaller when pronouncing 'ㅔ'.

Over time, the pronunciations have become similar, and most people cannot hear nor tell the difference between the two. As it is considered hard to distinguish 'ㅐ' and 'ㅔ' in their sounds by native speakers, when it's needed to specify which vowel usage, Koreans describe by breaking down letters by pieces.

See below for example:

$$\text{ㅐ} \quad = \quad \text{ㅏ} \quad + \quad \text{ㅣ}$$

[애]   [아]   [이]

$$\text{ㅔ} \quad = \quad \text{ㅓ} \quad + \quad \text{ㅣ}$$

[에]   [어]   [이]

Pronunciation		Tip for pronunciation
IPA	/a/	"a" as in "sp**a** /spɑː/"
Romanization	[a]	

Stroke order	Font variations	Letter creating principal
① ㅏ ②	아 아 아	ㅣ + ·

ㅏ
아
[a]

Example

아 가 나 다 랑 맘 받 샀

✏️ Trace & Learn

🔊 Track 01

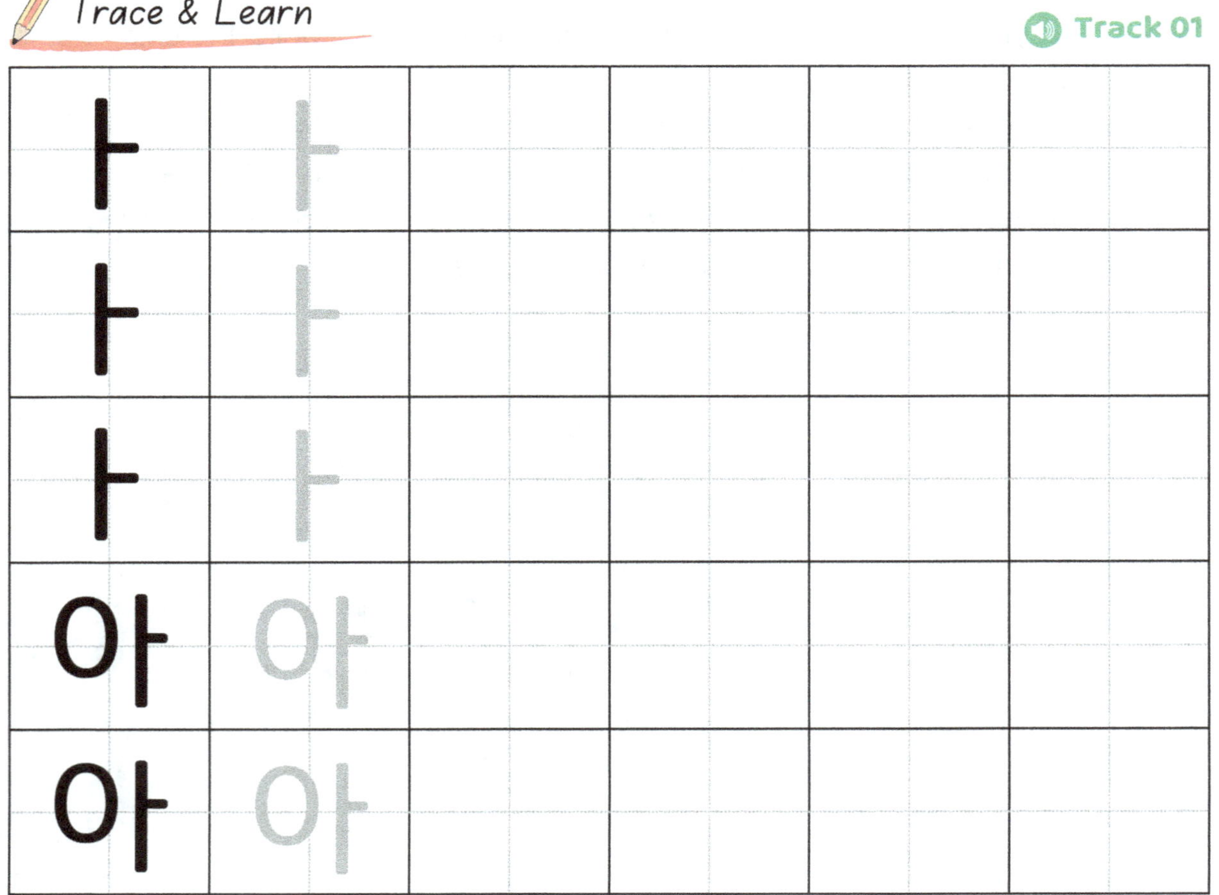

Pronunciation	Tip for pronunciation	
IPA /ʌ/ /ə/ Romanization [eo]	"u" as in "c<u>u</u>p /kʌp/"	
Stroke order	**Font variations**	**Letter creating principal**

ㅓ
어
[eo]

Example

어 거 너 더 럴 멈 벌 엋

✏️ *Trace & Learn*

🔊 **Track 02**

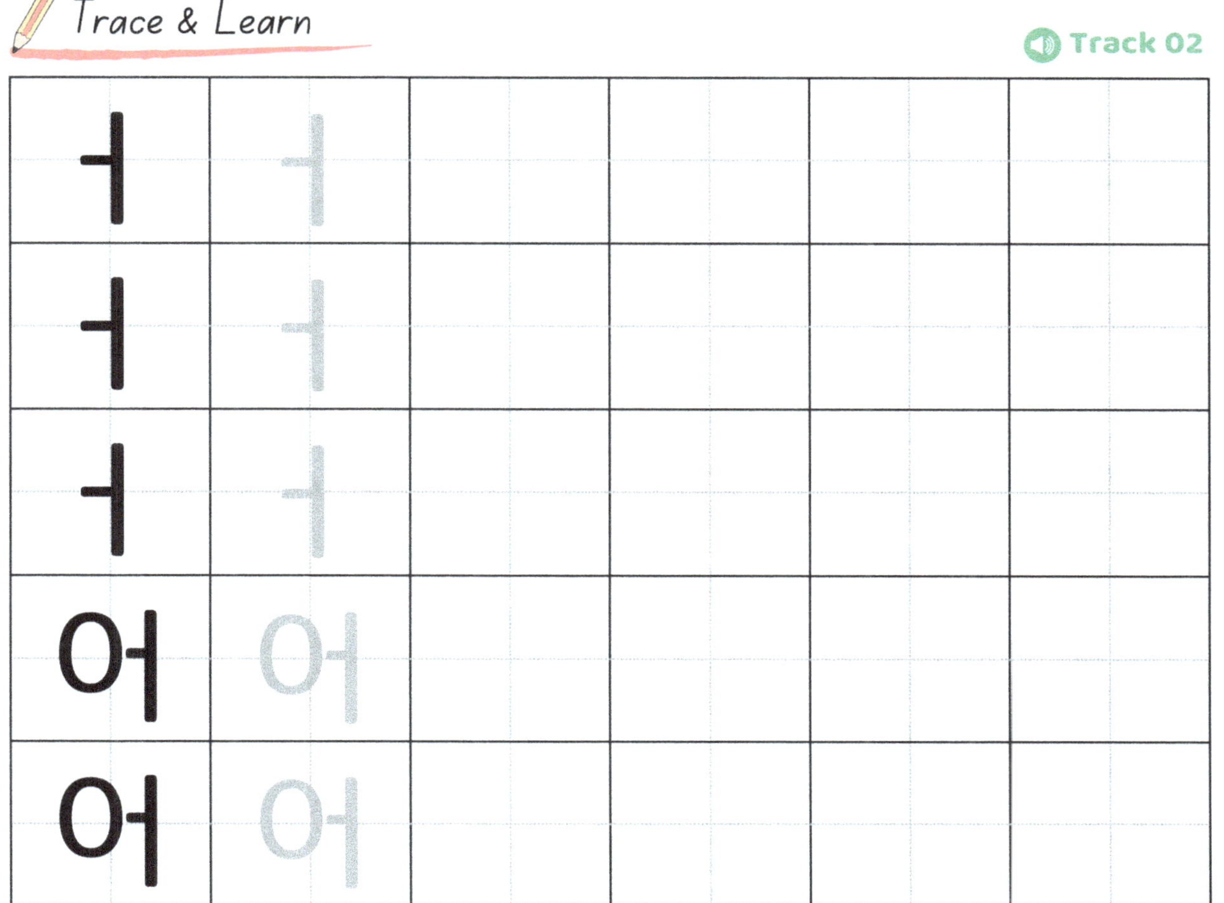

Pronunciation		Tip for pronunciation
IPA	/o/	"o" as in "**o**kay /oˈkʰeɪ/"
Romanization	[o]	

Stroke order	Font variations	Letter creating principal
	오 오 오	· + —

ㅗ
[o]

Example

오 고 노 도 롬 몰 봉 숙

✏️ Trace & Learn

🔊 Track 03

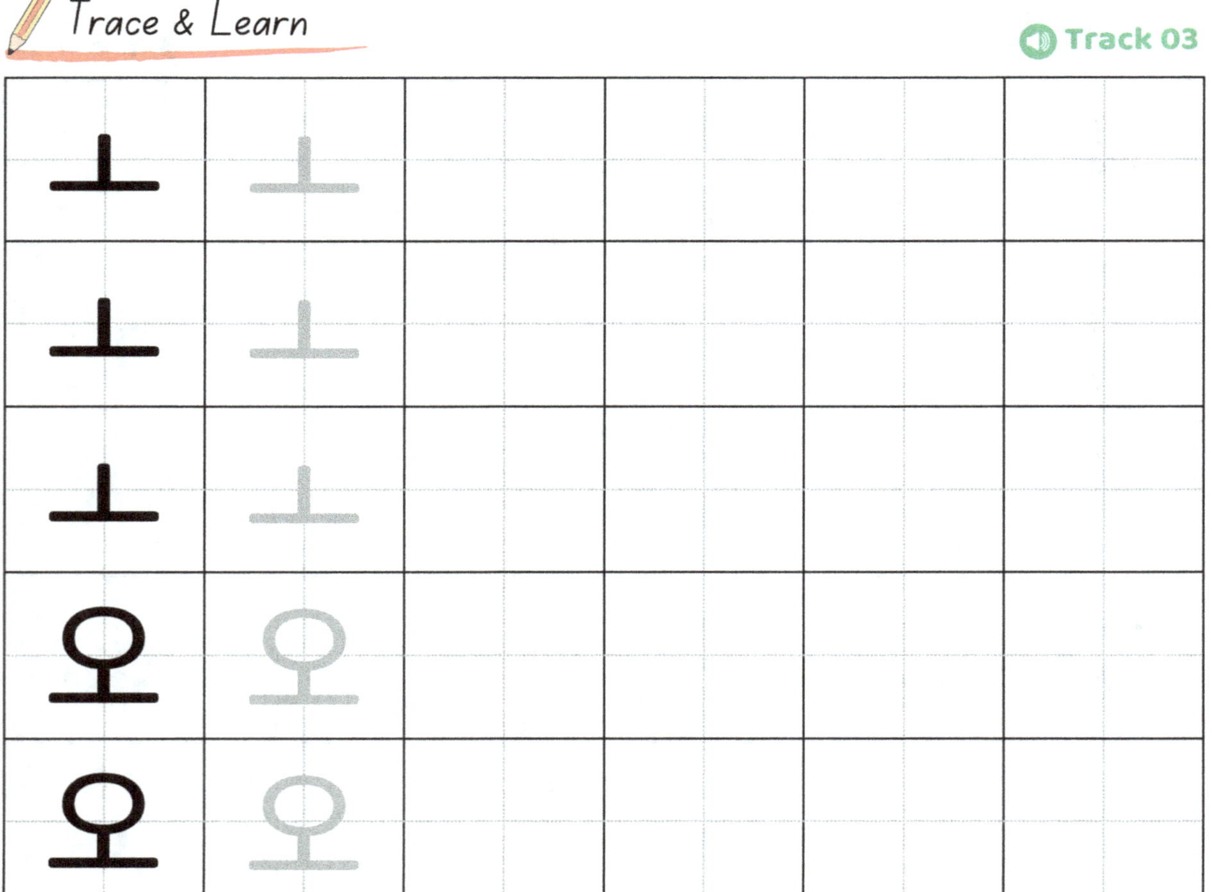

Pronunciation	Tip for pronunciation	
IPA /u/ /ʊ/ Romanization [u]	"oo" as in "sch<u>oo</u>l /ˈskuɫ/" or "g<u>oo</u>d /ˈɡʊd/"	

ㅜ
 우
 [u]

Stroke order	Font variations	Letter creating principal
	우 우 우	＿ + ·

Example

우 구 누 두 룰 문 붐 묵

🖍 *Trace & Learn*

🔊 **Track 04**

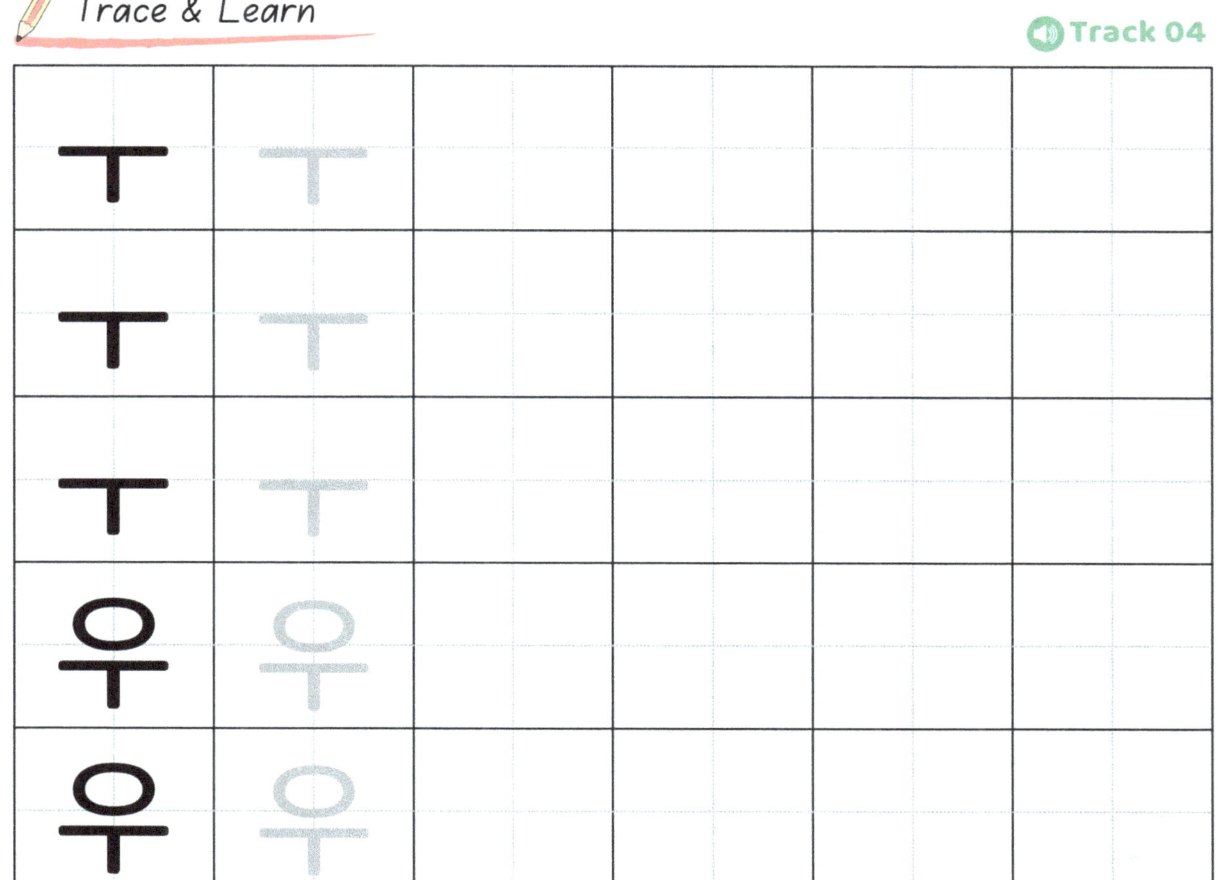

Pronunciation		Tip for pronunciation	
IPA	/ɯ/	This vowel is not found in English. Nevertheless, it is like pronouncing the vowel 'u' in 'p**u**t /pʊt/,' by opening your lips more horizontally.	
Romanization	[eu]		
Stroke order		**Font variations**	**Letter creating principal**
① →		으 으 으	━

Example

으 그 느 드 릉 믑 쁜 흑

Trace & Learn

🔊 Track 05

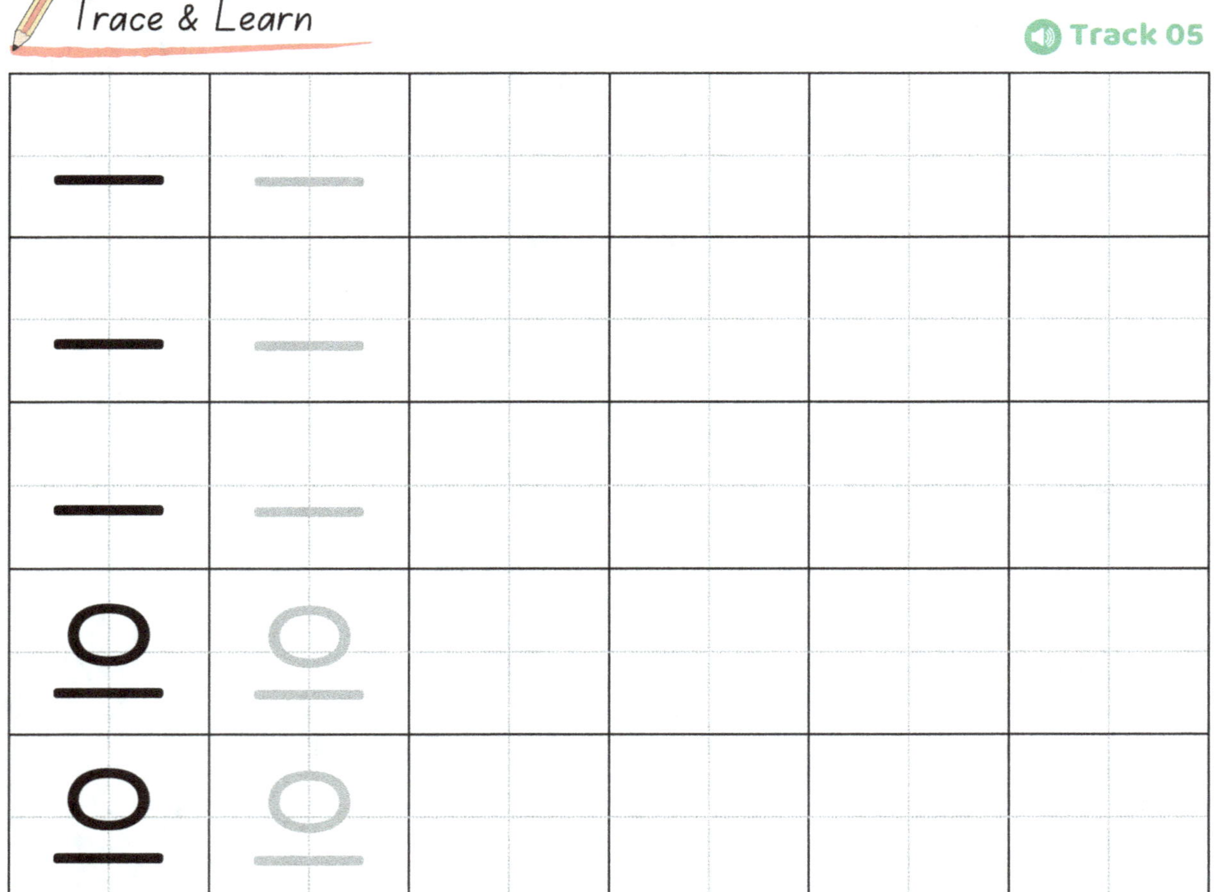

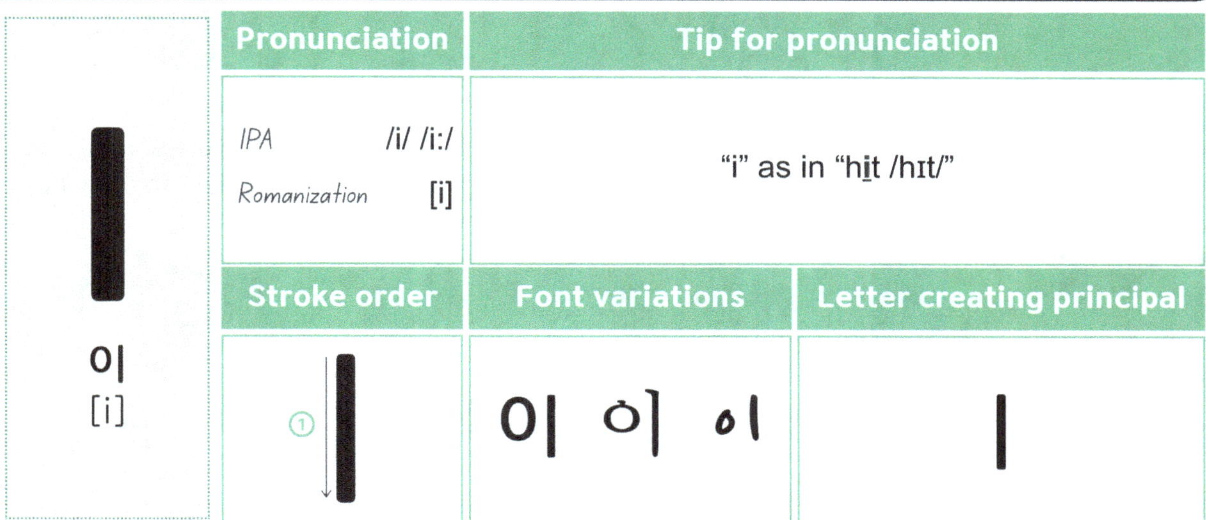

Pronunciation		Tip for pronunciation	
IPA	/i/ /iː/		
Romanization	[i]	"i" as in "h<u>i</u>t /hɪt/"	

Stroke order	Font variations	Letter creating principal
① ↓	이 이 이	ㅣ

이
[i]

Example

이 기 니 디 릴 밈 빗 싫

✏️ *Trace & Learn*

🔊 **Track 06**

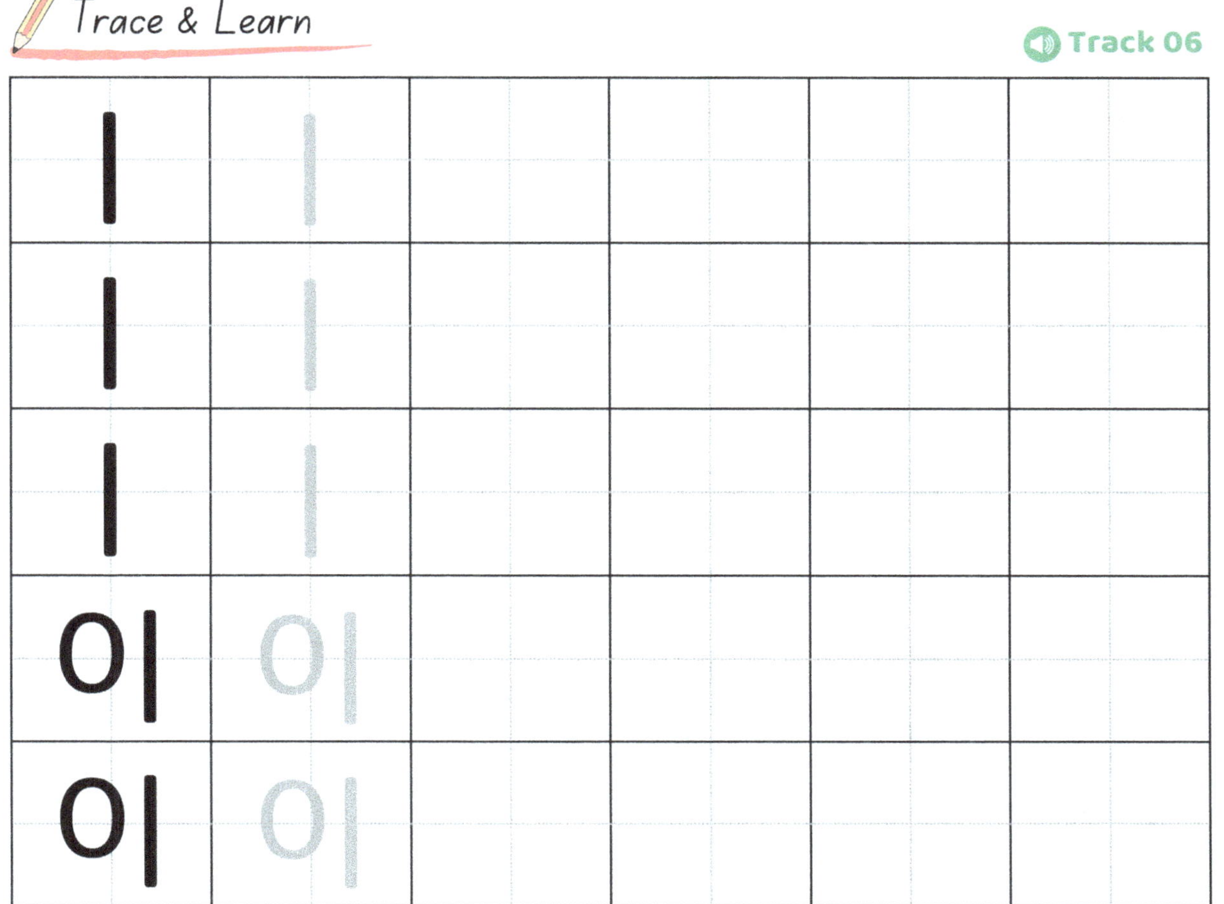

Pronunciation	Tip for pronunciation	
IPA /ɛ/ Romanization [ae]	"a" as in "c<u>a</u>t /kæt/" or "e" as in "b<u>e</u>d/bed/" ① This vowel and "ㅔ" are pronounced very similar. The size of the mouth opening is larger than when pronouncing "ㅔ"	
Stroke order	Font variations	Letter creating principal
	애 애 어	｜ + · · + ｜

ㅐ
애
[ae]

Example

애 개 내 대 햄 랫 뱀 생

✏️ *Trace & Learn*

🔊 **Track 07**

ㅔ
에
[e]

Pronunciation	Tip for pronunciation	
IPA /æ/ /e/ Romanization [e]	"a" as in "c**a**t /kæt/" or "e" as in "b**e**d/bed/" ① This vowel and "ㅐ" are pronounced very similar. The size of the mouth opening is smaller than when pronouncing "ㅐ"	
Stroke order	**Font variations**	**Letter creating principal**
① → ② ③ ㅔ	에 에 에	· + ㅣ + ㅣ

Example

에 게 네 데 켈 멤 벳 셍

✏️ Trace & Learn

🔊 **Track 08**

다음 글자를 써보세요.
Practice writing the letters below.

Letter	Pronun-ciation	Writing Practice				
ㅏ	/a/	ㅏ	ㅏ			
ㅓ	/ʌ/ /ə/	ㅓ	ㅓ			
ㅗ	/o/	ㅗ	ㅗ			
ㅜ	/u/ /ʊ/	ㅜ	ㅜ			
ㅡ	/ɯ/	ㅡ	ㅡ			
ㅣ	/i/ /iː/	ㅣ	ㅣ			
ㅐ	/ɛ/	ㅐ	ㅐ			
ㅔ	/æ/ /e/	ㅔ	ㅔ			

1

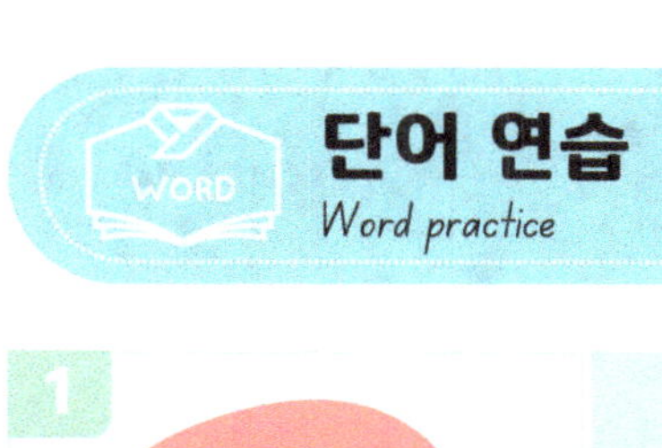

이　이

Two
(Sino number system)

2

오　오

Five
(Sino number system)

3

아　이　아　이

Kid, Child

4

오　이

Cucumber

1. 다음 글자를 잘 듣고 소리 내어 읽어보세요.

Listen carefully and read out loud the following letters.

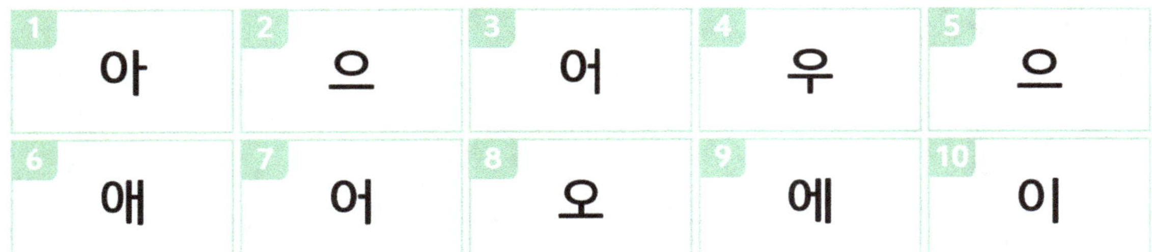

| 1 아 | 2 으 | 3 어 | 4 우 | 5 으 |
| 6 애 | 7 어 | 8 오 | 9 에 | 10 이 |

2. 다음을 잘 듣고 맞으면 O표, 틀리면 X표를 하세요.

Listen carefully and mark O for correct or X for incorrect.

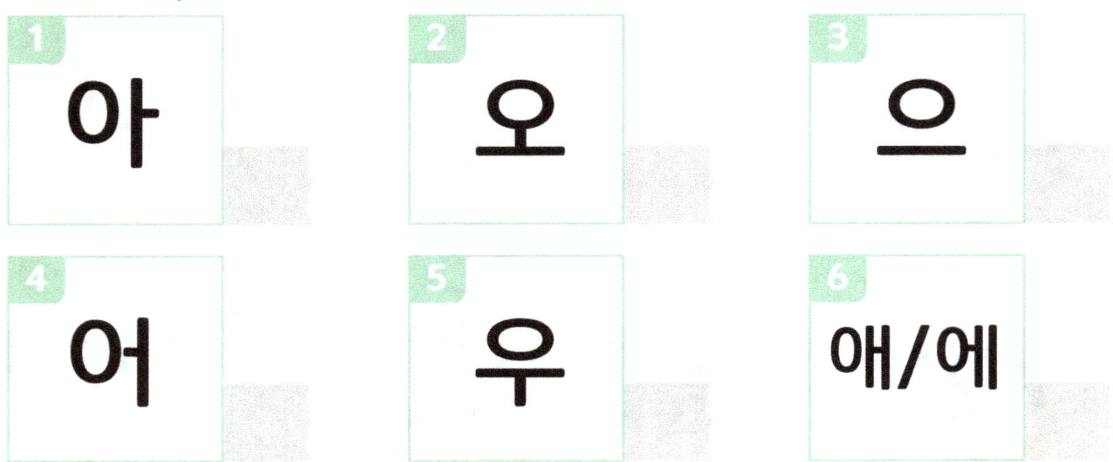

| 1 아 | 2 오 | 3 으 |
| 4 어 | 5 우 | 6 애/에 |

3. 잘 듣고 맞는 글자에 O표 하세요.

Listen carefully and mark O on the correct letter.

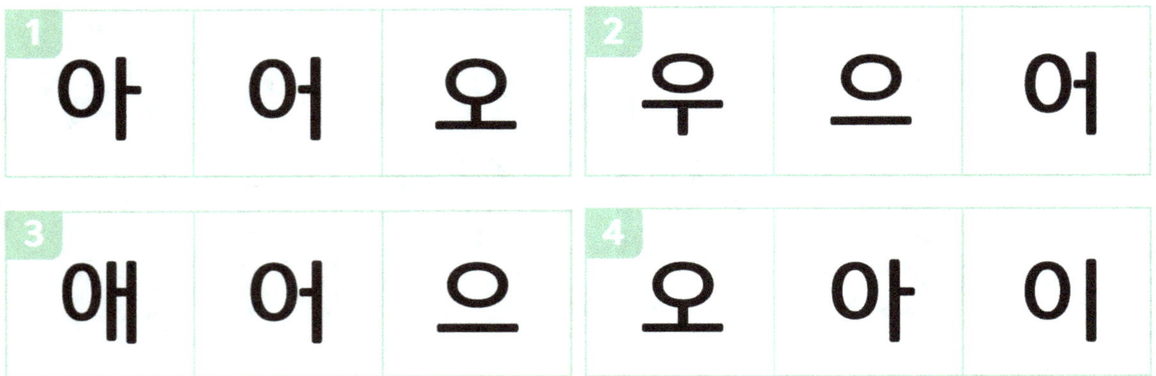

| 1 아 어 오 | 2 우 으 어 |
| 3 애 어 으 | 4 오 아 이 |

4. 잘 듣고 단어를 받아쓰세요.

Listen carefully and dictate the word.

5. 다음 그림에 알맞은 단어를 쓰세요.

Write the matched word under the picture.

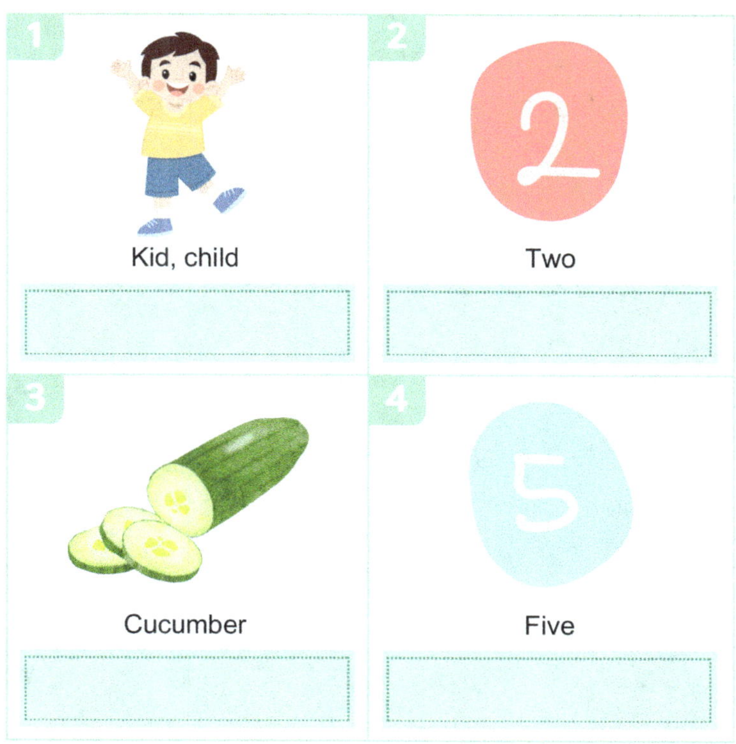

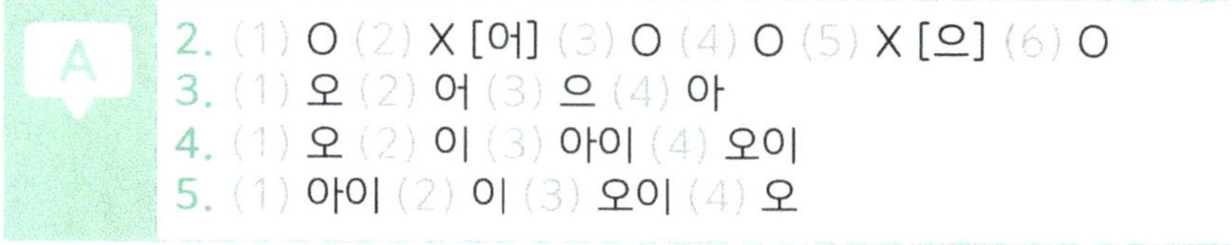

2. Single Consonant

단자음

The consonant is the sound that is met with an interruption /blockage in one of our vocal organs, such as 'b, c, d, and the rest' in English. For example, when you pronounce 마[ma], your lips(vocal organ) close to giving an interruption to the sound. In Korean, there are fourteen (14) single consonants. Keep in mind that the letters' shapes can vary depending on the fonts and the position of a syllable. (To see the details, refer to pages 36-63)

Korean single consonants *Pronunciation: /IPA/*

Conso-nant	ㄱ	ㄴ	ㄷ	ㄹ	ㅁ	ㅂ	ㅅ
Name	기역 [gi-yeok]	니은 [ni-eun]	디귿 [di-geut]	리을 [ri-eul]	미음 [mi-eum]	비읍 [bi-eup]	시옷 [si-ot]
Pronun-ciation	/g/ /k/	/n/	/d/ /t/	/r/ /l/	/m/	/b/ /p/	/s/
Conso-nant	ㅇ	ㅈ	ㅊ	ㅋ	ㅌ	ㅍ	ㅎ
Name	이응 [i-eung]	지읒 [ji-eut]	치읓 [chi-eut]	키읔 [ki-euk]	티읕 [ti-eut]	피읖 [pi-eup]	히읗 [hi-eut]
Pronun-ciation	silent	/tʃ/ /dʒ/	/tʃʰ/	/kʰ/	/tʰ/	/pʰ/	/h/

The close relationship between consonants

The four consonants below in green are formed based on the other consonants in yellow to reflect more wind pressure, which you may notice from the similar shape between the two. Thus, you can remember letters easily if you understand the principles of creating Hangul(Page 11) and the correlation between similar consonants.

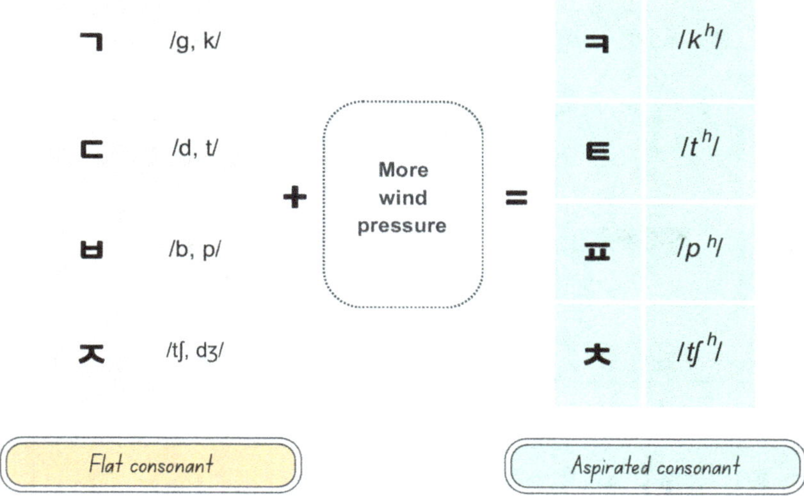

How to pronounce aspirated consonant accurately?

- **Adding wind pressure**: Aspirated consonants' pronunciations need more wind pressure. Hold a tissue in front of your mouth, and pronounce each consonant, and see the airflow of these consonants. Then, you will notice the intense movement of the tissue when you pronounce aspirated ones. (Refer to the video 2. Single Consonant)
- **Using a higher pitch**: Aspirated consonants are pronounced with a higher pitch tone compared to flat consonants.

Remember each consonant's name!

Each Korean consonant has a particular name to refer to, like the English alphabet (i.e., B[bee]). Knowing their names is indispensable because no Koreans can understand if you describe them from the English perspective. (i.e., 'ㄴ' as 'n' sounding consonant) This is because Koreans do not learn Hangul through associations with English.

There's a tip you can use to memorize them more easily. **All names start and end with its consonant, and the first vowel is 'ㅣ' and the next one is 'ㅡ'** except for 'ㄱ(기역), ㄷ(디귿), ㅅ(시옷)'

Pronunciation	Tip for pronunciation
IPA /g/ /k/ Romanization [g] [k]	"g" as in "**g**un/gʌn/" or "**g**ift/gɪft/"

Stroke order	Font variations
	가　가　가　가

ㄱ

기역
[gi-yeok]

Example

가 거 고 구 그 기 객 곽

✏️ Trace & Learn

🔊 **Track 11**

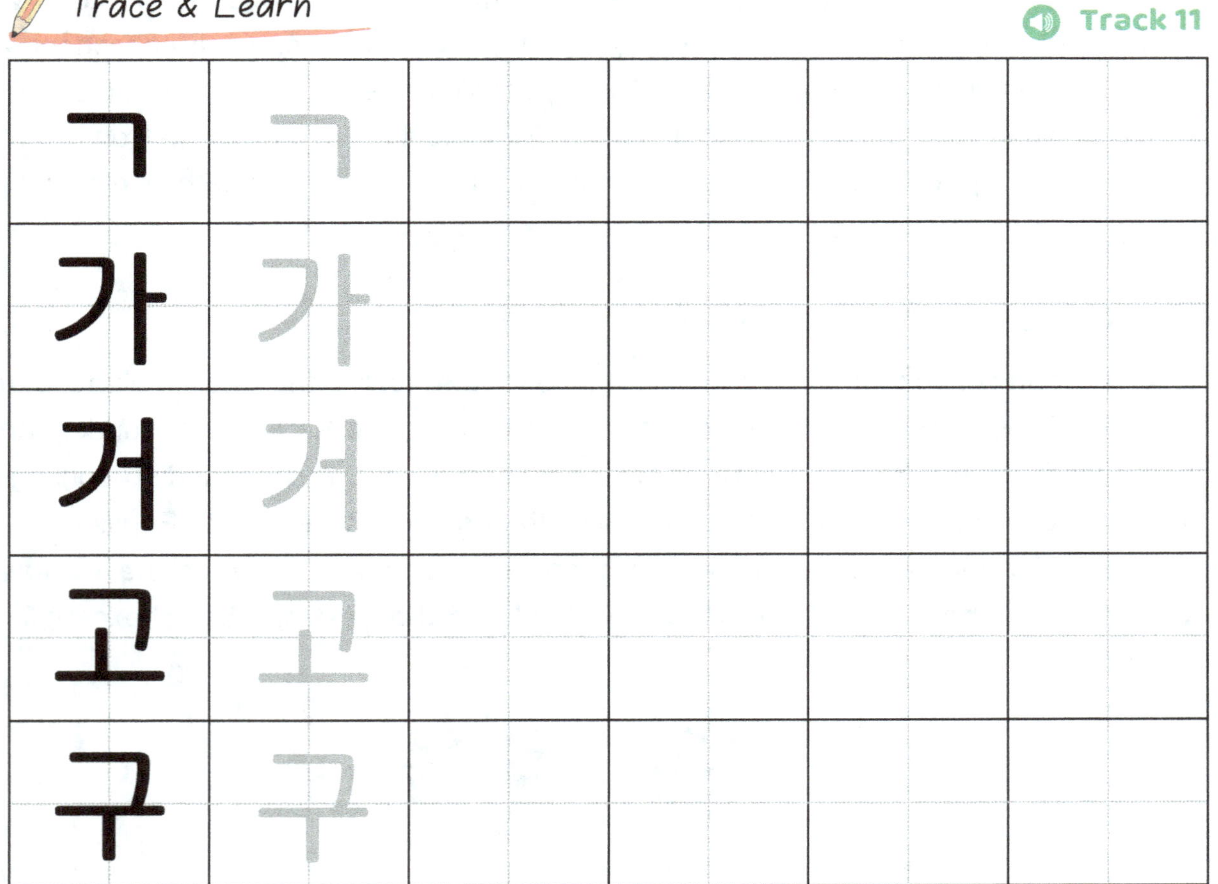

1

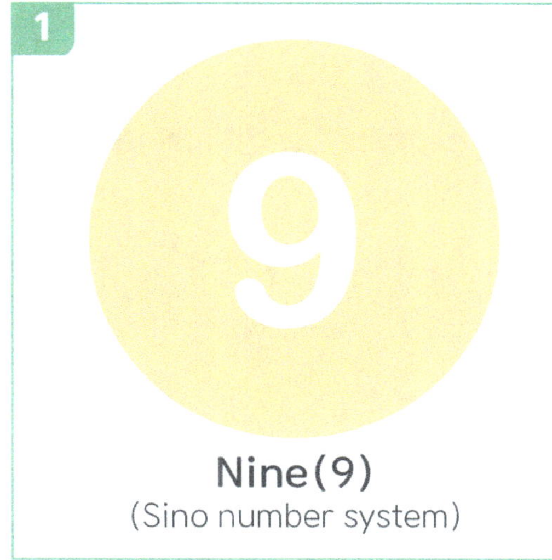

Nine(9)
(Sino number system)

구

2

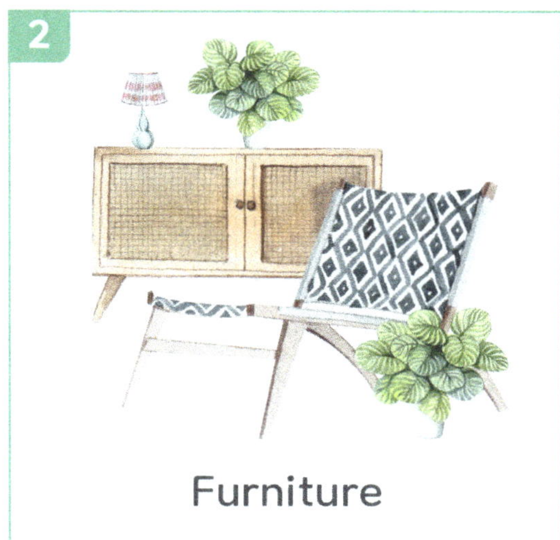

Furniture

가 구

3

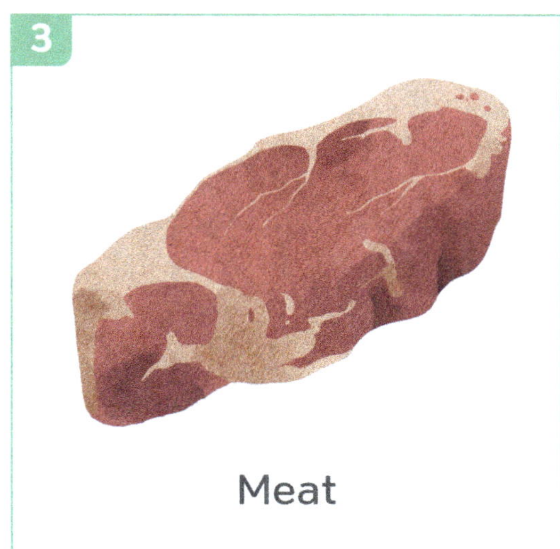

Meat

고 기

Pronunciation		Tip for pronunciation
IPA /n/ Romanization [n]		"n" as in "**n**ose/noʊz/" or "**n**ame/neɪm/"
Stroke order		**Font variations**
 ① ㄴ		나 나 나 나

ㄴ

니은
[ni-eun]

Example

나 너 노 누 느 니 낸 넨

✏️ Trace & Learn

🔊 **Track 12**

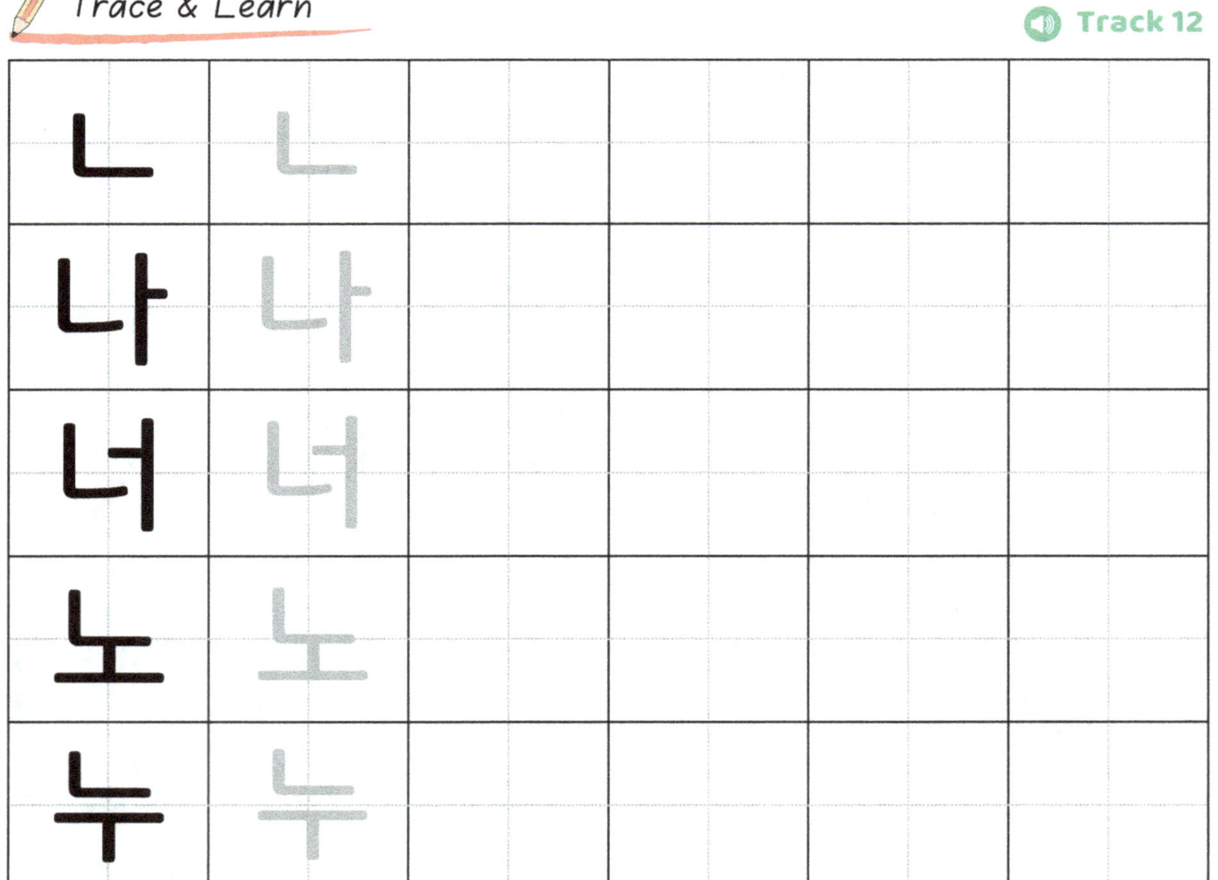

ㄴ ㄴ

나 나

너 너

노 노

누 누

1

I, Me

나 나

2

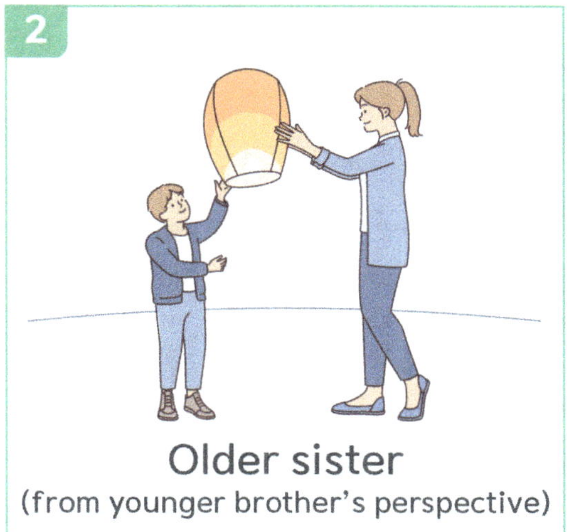

Older sister
(from younger brother's perspective)

누 나 누 나

3

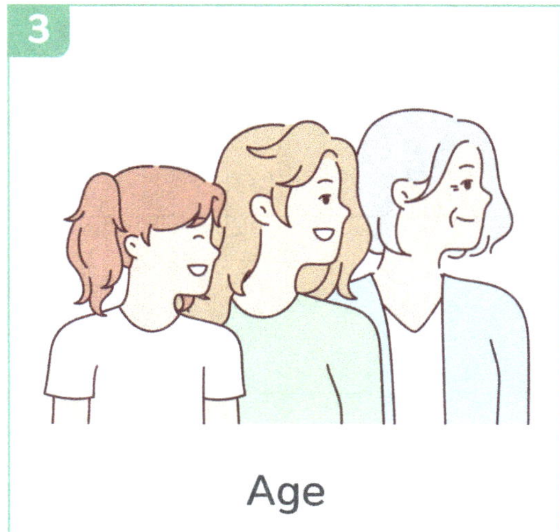

Age

나 이 나 이

ㄷ

디귿
[di-geuk]

Pronunciation	Tip for pronunciation
IPA /d/, /t/ Romanization [d], [t]	"d" as in "**d**ance /dæns/" or "**d**oor /dɔː(r)/"

Stroke order	Font variations
① → ② → ㄷ	다 다 다 다

Example

다 더 도 두 드 디 닫 들

✏️ Trace & Learn

🔊 **Track 13**

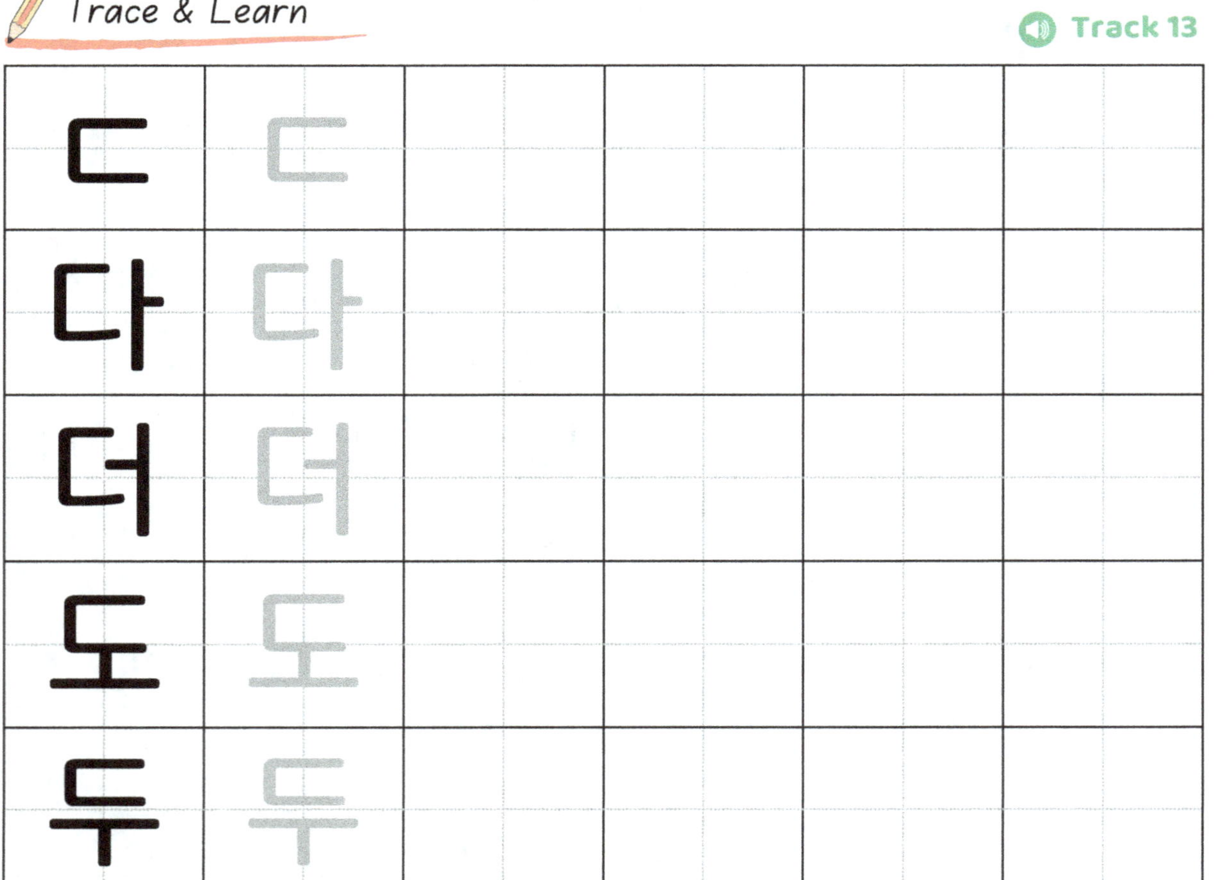

1

More

더 더

2

Soy milk

두 유 두 유

3

Pray

기 도 기 도

	ㄹ
리을 [ri-eul]	

Pronunciation	Tip for pronunciation
IPA /r/, /l/ Romanization [r], [l]	Similar to "r" as in "<u>r</u>ice /raɪs/" ⓘ Pronounce it by lightly touching the roof of your mouth (in the middle between your palate and your gum) with your tongue tip.

Stroke order	Font variations
ㄹ ① ② ③	라 라 라 라

Example

라 러 로 루 르 리 랠 렐

✏️ Trace & Learn

🔊 **Track 14**

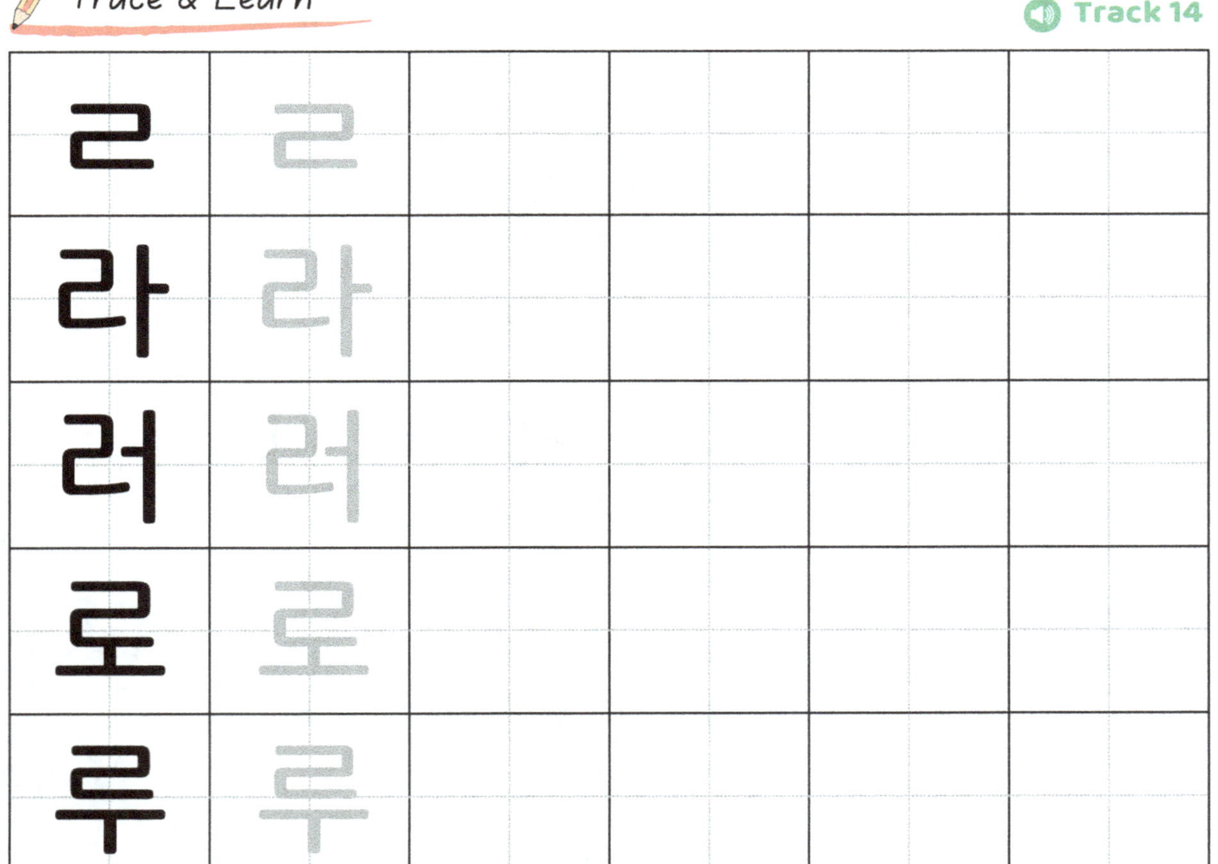

1

Country, Nation

나 라 나 라

2

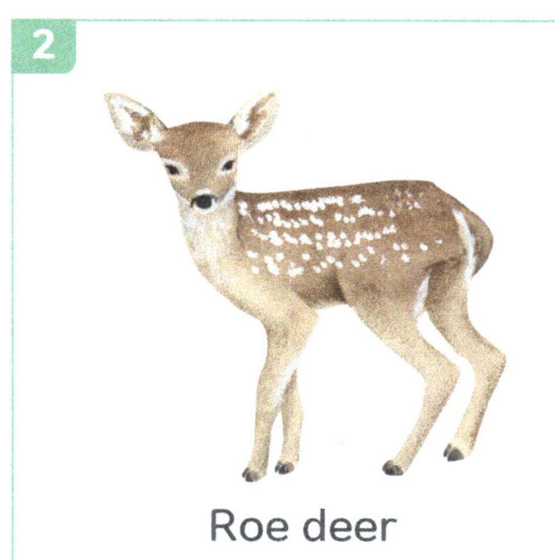

Roe deer

노 루 노 루

3

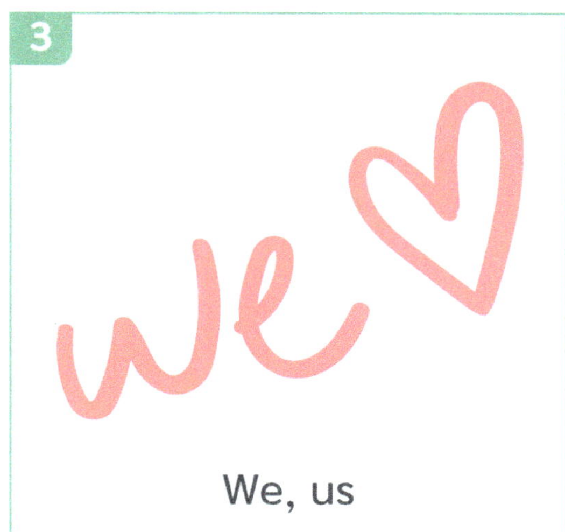

We, us

우 리 우 리

Pronunciation	Tip for pronunciation
IPA /m/ Romanization [m]	"m" as in "**m**ilk /mɪlk/" or "**m**ind /maɪnd/"
Stroke order	Font variations
① ② ③	마 마 마 마

ㅁ

미음
[mi-eum]

Example

마 머 모 무 므 미 맴 멤

✏️ Trace & Learn

🔊 **Track 15**

ㅁ	ㅁ				
마	마				
머	머				
모	모				
우	우				

1

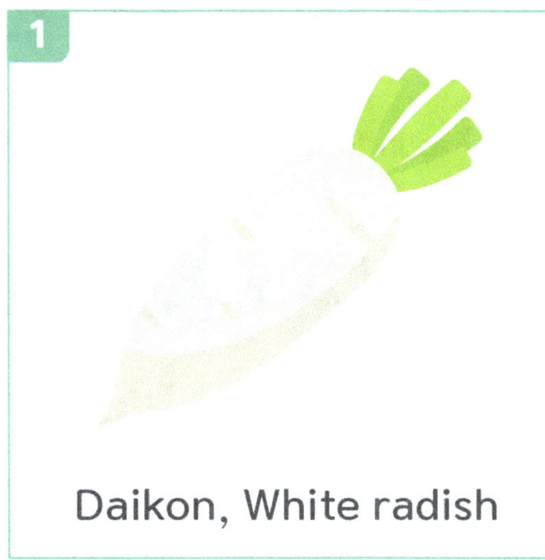

Daikon, White radish

무 무

2

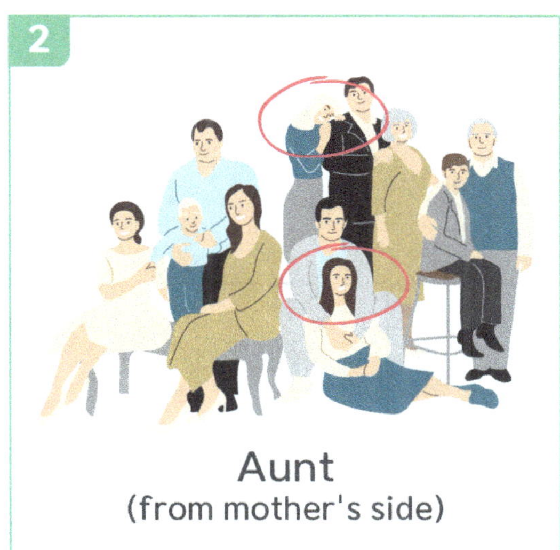

Aunt
(from mother's side)

이 모 이 모

3

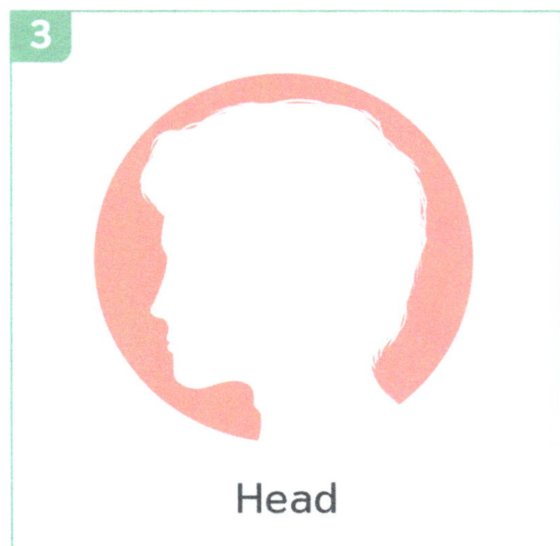

Head

머 리 머 리

ㅂ

비읍
[bi-eup]

Pronunciation	Tip for pronunciation
IPA /b/ /p/ *Romanization* [b] [p]	"b" as in "**b**oy /bɔɪ/"

Stroke order	Font variations
	바 바 바 바

Example

바 버 보 부 브 비 뱁 벱

 Trace & Learn

Track 16

1

Rain

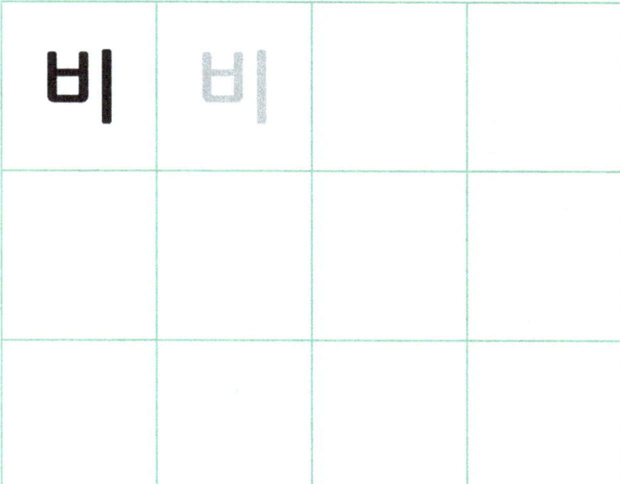

비 | 비 | | |

2

Sea, Ocean

바 | 다 | 바 | 다

3

Married couple

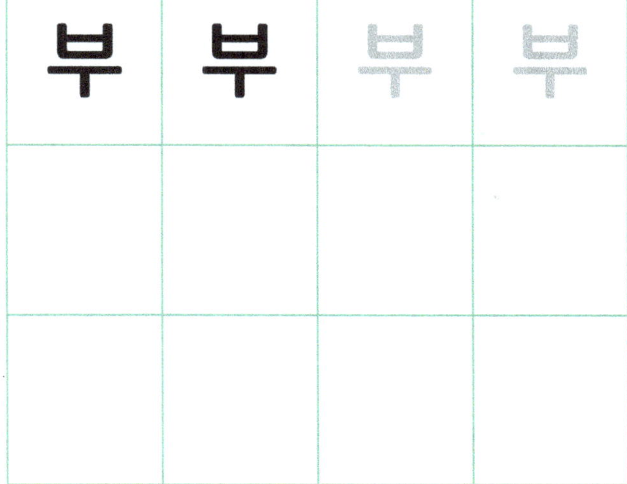

부 | 부 | 부 | 부

Pronunciation		Tip for pronunciation
IPA	/s/	"s" as in "**s**ky /skaɪ/" (!) However, when 'ㅅ' is followed by the vowels "ㅑ, ㅕ, ㅛ, ㅠ, ㅖ, ㅒ, and ㅖ," it's pronounced "sh" /ʃ/ as in **sh**oes /ʃuː/
Romanization	[s]	

ㅅ

시옷
[si-ot]

Stroke order	Font variations
① ㅅ ②	사 사 사 사

Example

사 서 소 수 스 시 샛 셋

✏️ Trace & Learn

🔊 **Track 17**

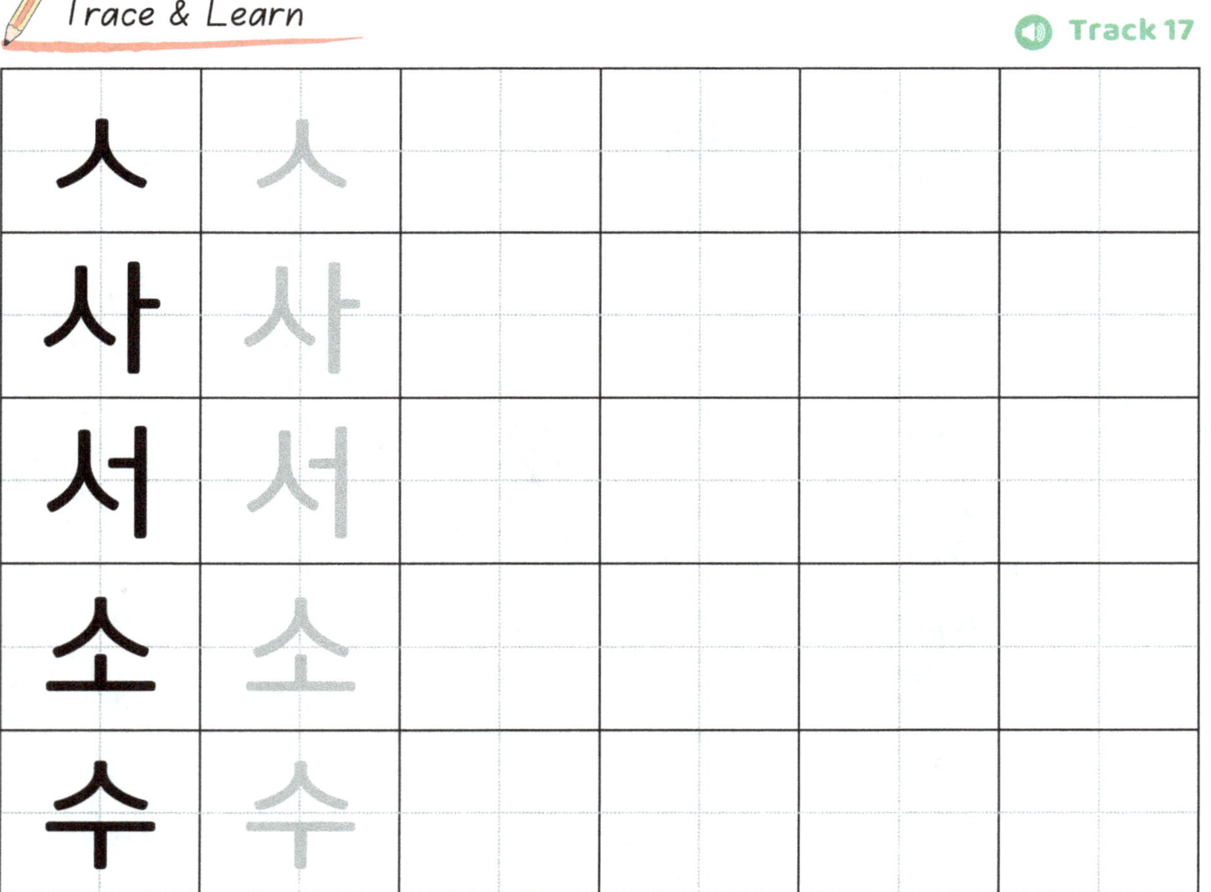

1

Cow

소	소		

2

City

도	시	도	시

3

Singer

가	수	가	수

Pronunciation	Tip for pronunciation
Silent consonant	"Silent h" as in "<u>h</u>onest /ˈɑː.nɪst/" or "<u>h</u>our /aʊr/"

Stroke order	Font variations
 ①	아 아 아 아

ㅇ

이응
[i-eung]

Example

아 어 오 우 으 이 앵 엥

✏️ Trace & Learn

🔊 **Track 18**

1

Baby

| 아 | 기 | 아 | 기 |

2

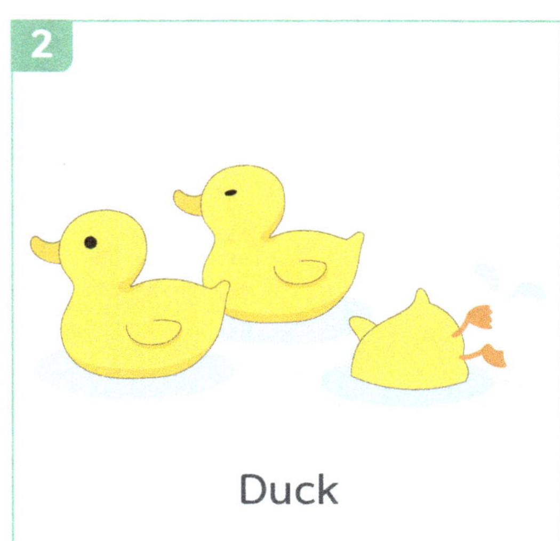

Duck

| 오 | 리 | 오 | 리 |

3

Moving

| 이 | 사 | 이 | 사 |

ㅈ

지읒
[ji-eut]

Pronunciation	Tip for pronunciation
IPA /tʃ/ /dʒ/ Romanization [j]	"j" as in "**j**uice /dʒuːs/" or "**j**am /dʒæm/"

Stroke order	Font variations
ㅈ ① ②	자　자　자　자 Common digital font　　　Common handwriting font

Example

자 저 조 주 즈 지 젖 짖

✎ Trace & Learn

🔊 **Track 19**

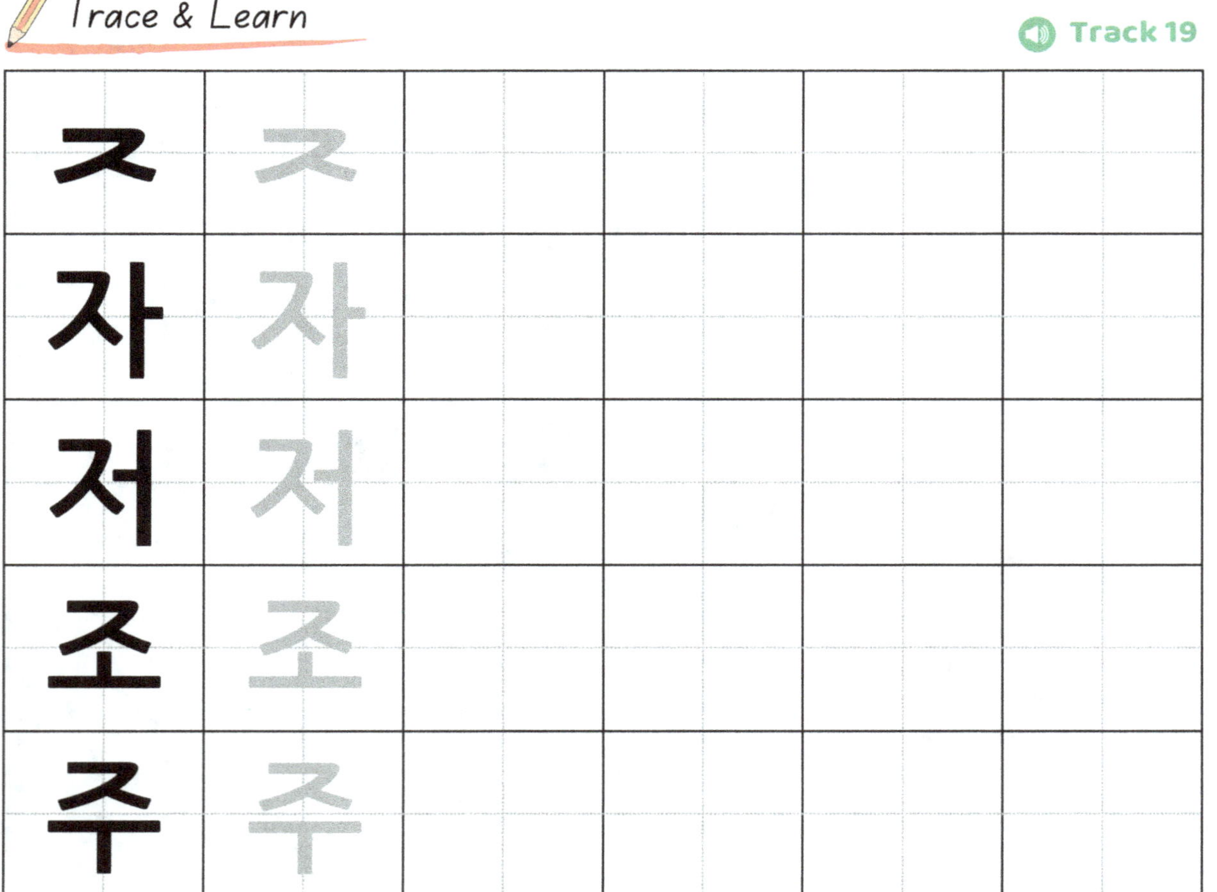

ㅈ	ㅈ				
자	자				
저	저				
조	조				
주	주				

1

Juice

주 스

2

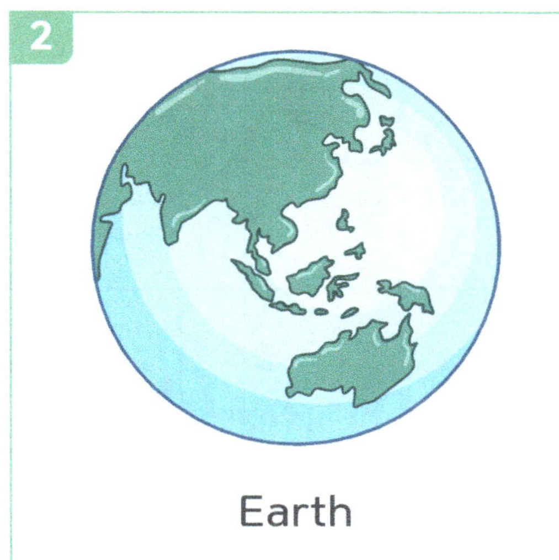

Earth

지 구

3

Rich, wealthy person

부 자

Pronunciation		Tip for pronunciation
IPA	/tʃʰ/	"ch" as in "**ch**air /tʃer/" or "**ch**ild /tʃaɪld/"
Romanization	[ch]	

ㅊ

치읓
[chi-eut]

Stroke order	Font variations

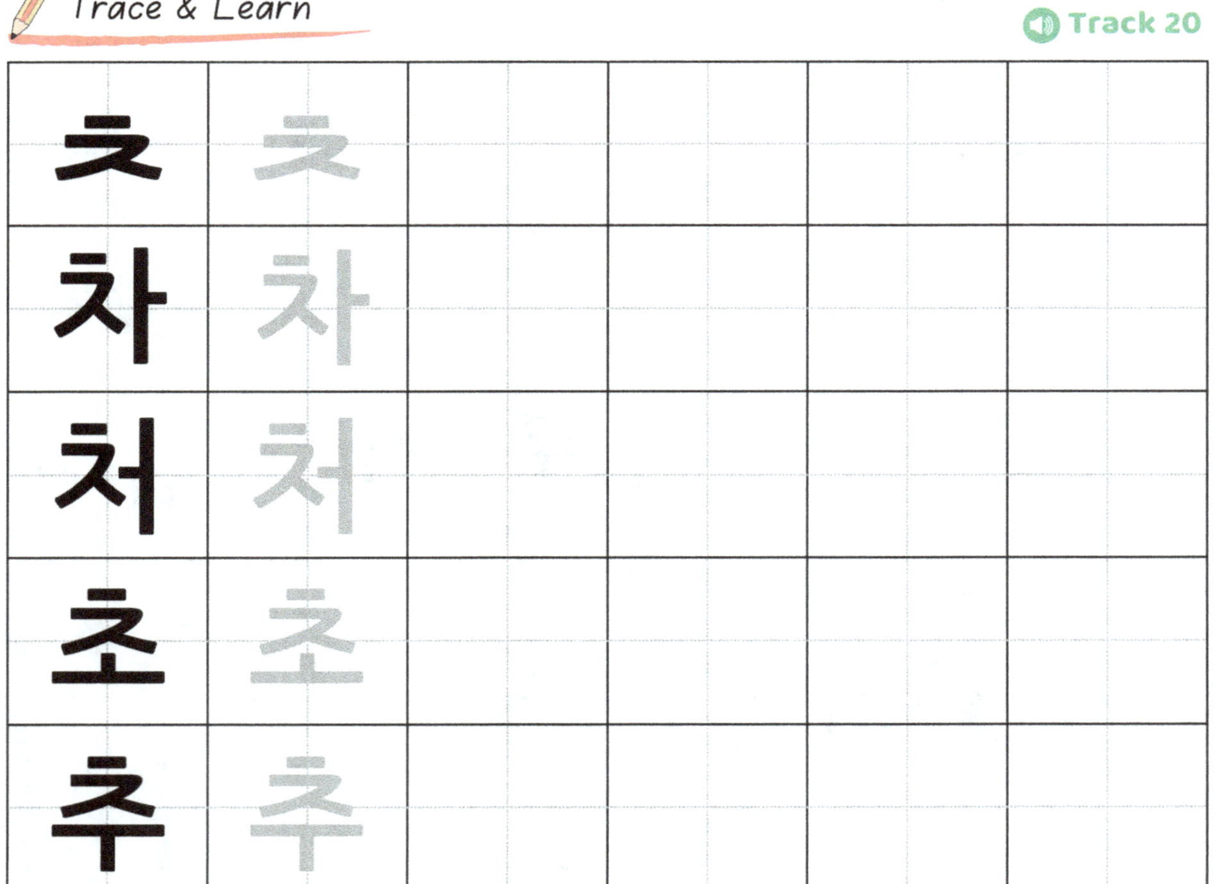

Example

차 처 초 추 츠 치 숯 빛

✏️ *Trace & Learn*

🔊 **Track 20**

ㅊ	ㅊ				
차	차				
처	처				
초	초				
추	추				

1

Car / Tea

차　차

2

Skirt

치 마　치 마

3

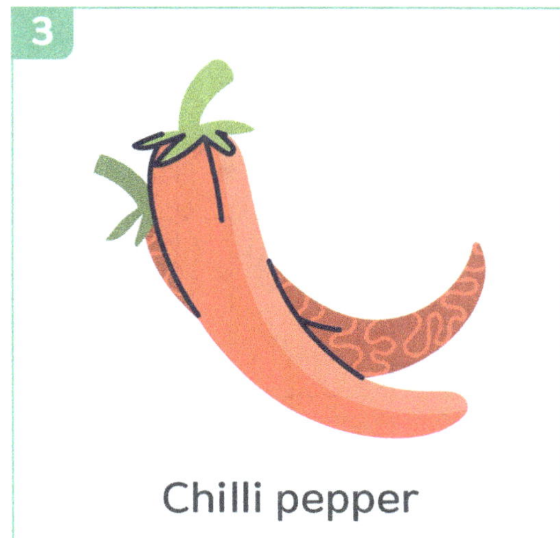

Chilli pepper

고 추　고 추

Pronunciation		Tip for pronunciation
IPA	/kʰ/	"k" as in "**k**ey /kiː/" or "**k**orea /kəríːə/"
Romanization	[k]	

ㅋ

키읔
[ki-euk]

Stroke order	Font variations
	카 카 카 카

Example

카 커 코 쿠 크 키 얶 읔

✏️ Trace & Learn

🔊 **Track 21**

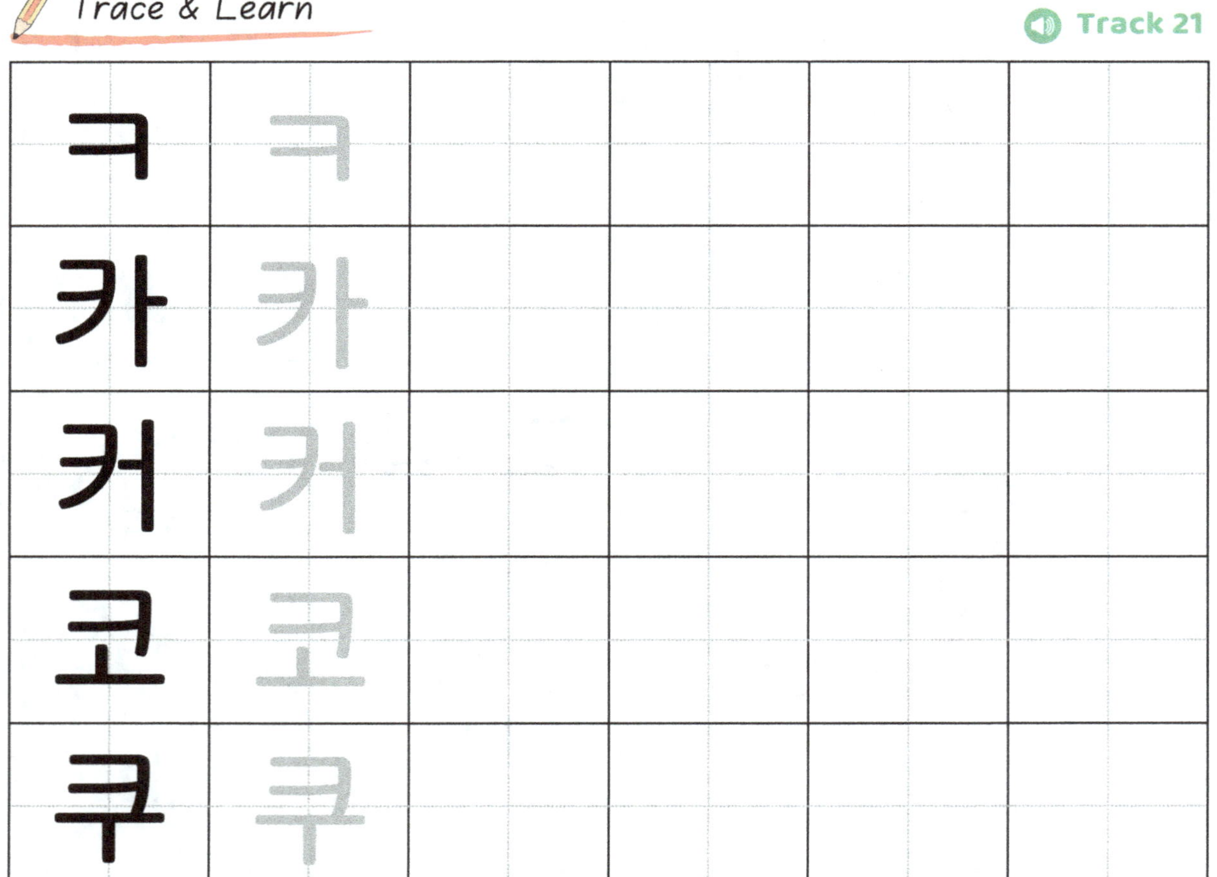

ㅋ	ㅋ			
카	카			
커	커			
코	코			
쿠	쿠			

1

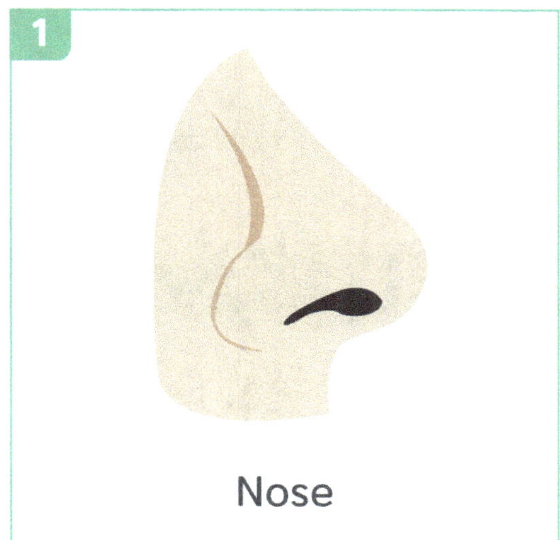

Nose

코 코

2

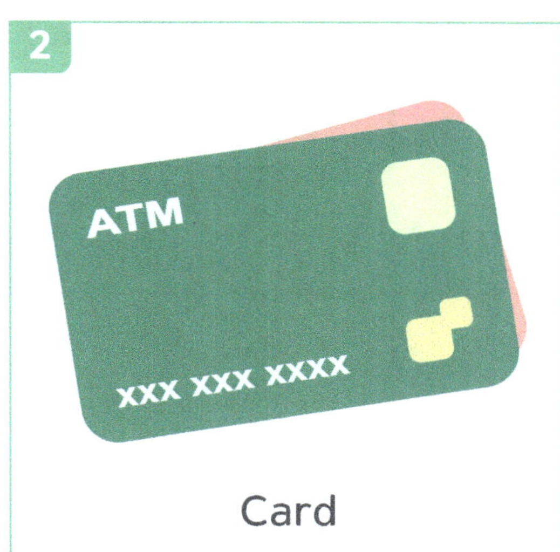

Card

카 드 카 드

3

Cookie

쿠 키 쿠 키

Pronunciation	Tip for pronunciation
IPA /tʰ/ Romanization [t]	"t" as in "**t**ree /triː/" or "**t**axi /ˈtæksi/"

Stroke order	Font variations
	타 타 타 타

ㅌ
티읕
[ti-eut]

Example

타 터 토 투 트 티 같 밑

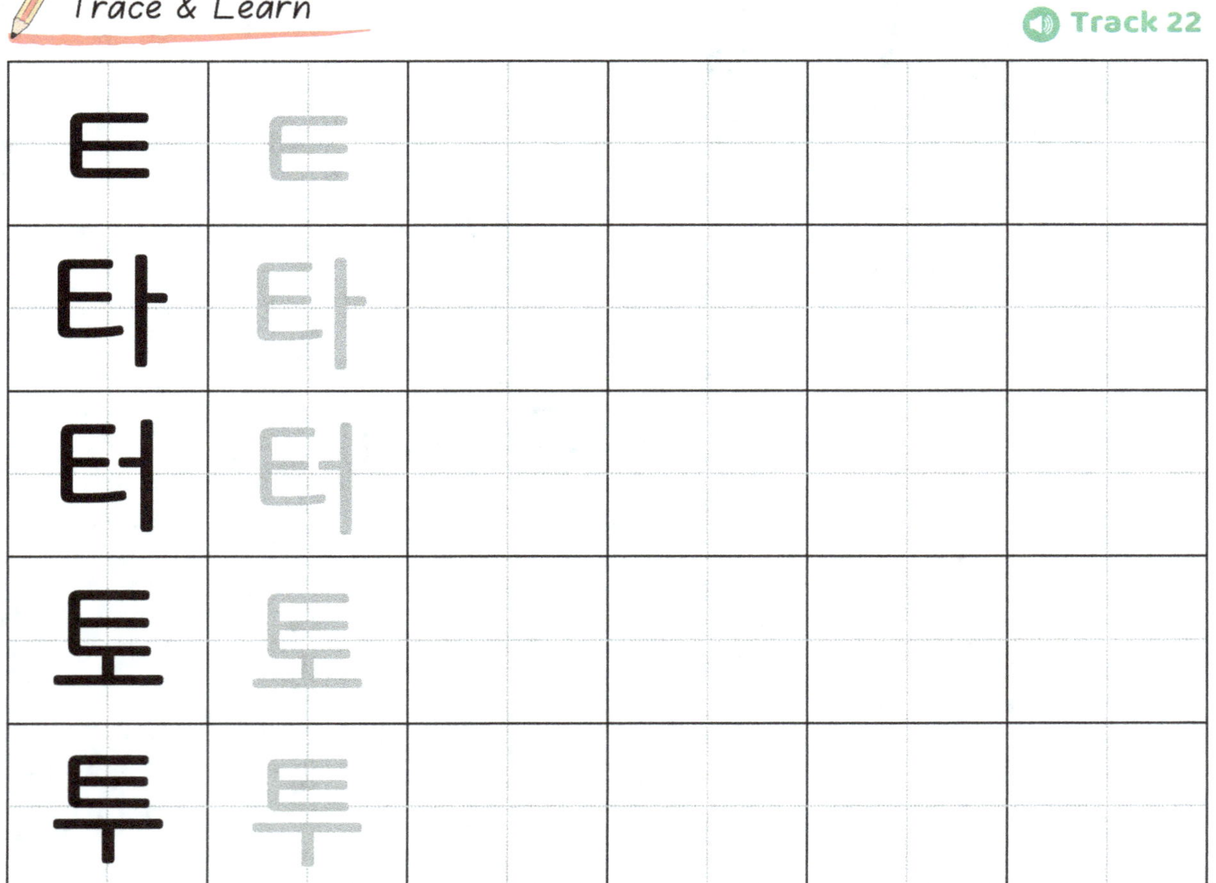

✏️ *Trace & Learn* 🔊 **Track 22**

1

Ostrich

타 조 타 조

2

Guitar

기 타 기 타

3

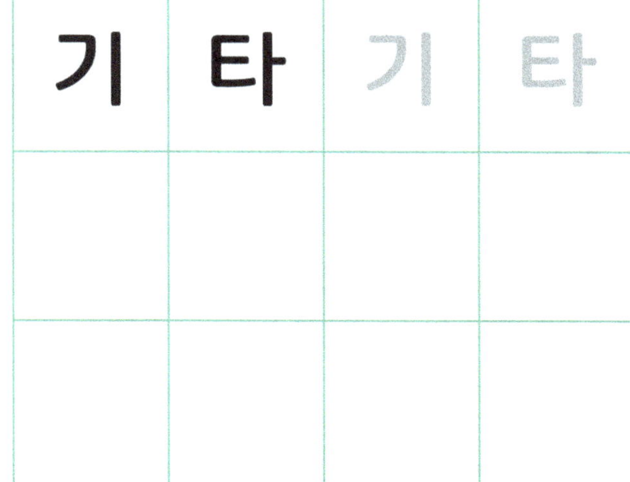

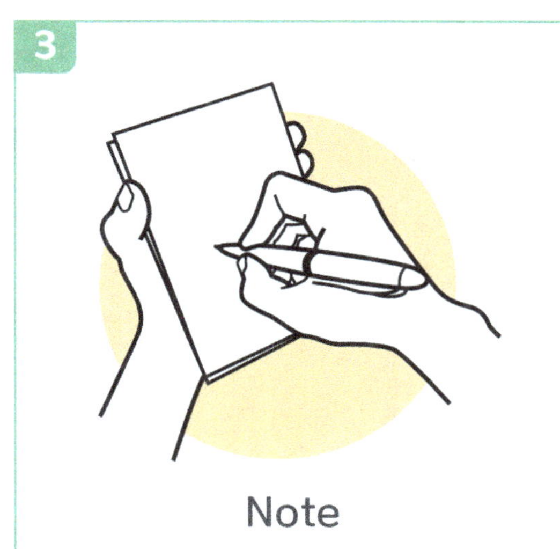

Note

노 트 노 트

Pronunciation	Tip for pronunciation
IPA /pʰ/ Romanization [p]	"p" as in "pen /pen/" or "power /ˈpaʊ.ɚ/"

Stroke order	Font variations
	파 파 파 파

ㅍ
피읖
[pi-eup]

Example

파 퍼 포 푸 프 피 앞 숲

✏️ *Trace & Learn*

🔊 **Track 23**

1

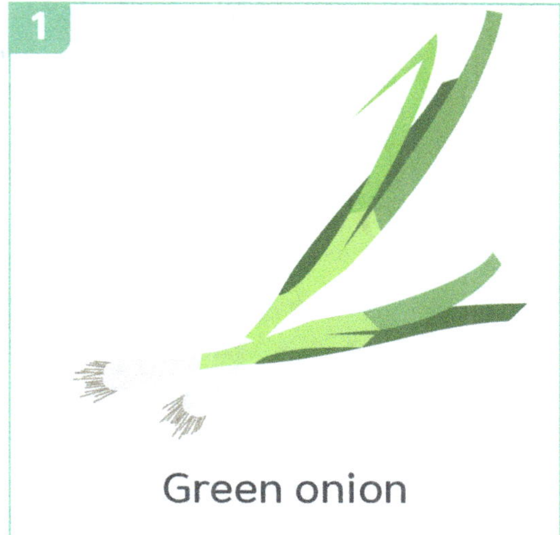

Green onion

파 파

2

Grapes

포 도 포 도

3

Piri (Korean pan pipe)

피 리 피 리

Pronunciation	Tip for pronunciation
IPA /h/ Romanization [h]	"h" as in "**h**at /hæt/" or "**h**ouse /haʊz/"
Stroke order	Font variations

ㅎ
히읗
[hi-eut]

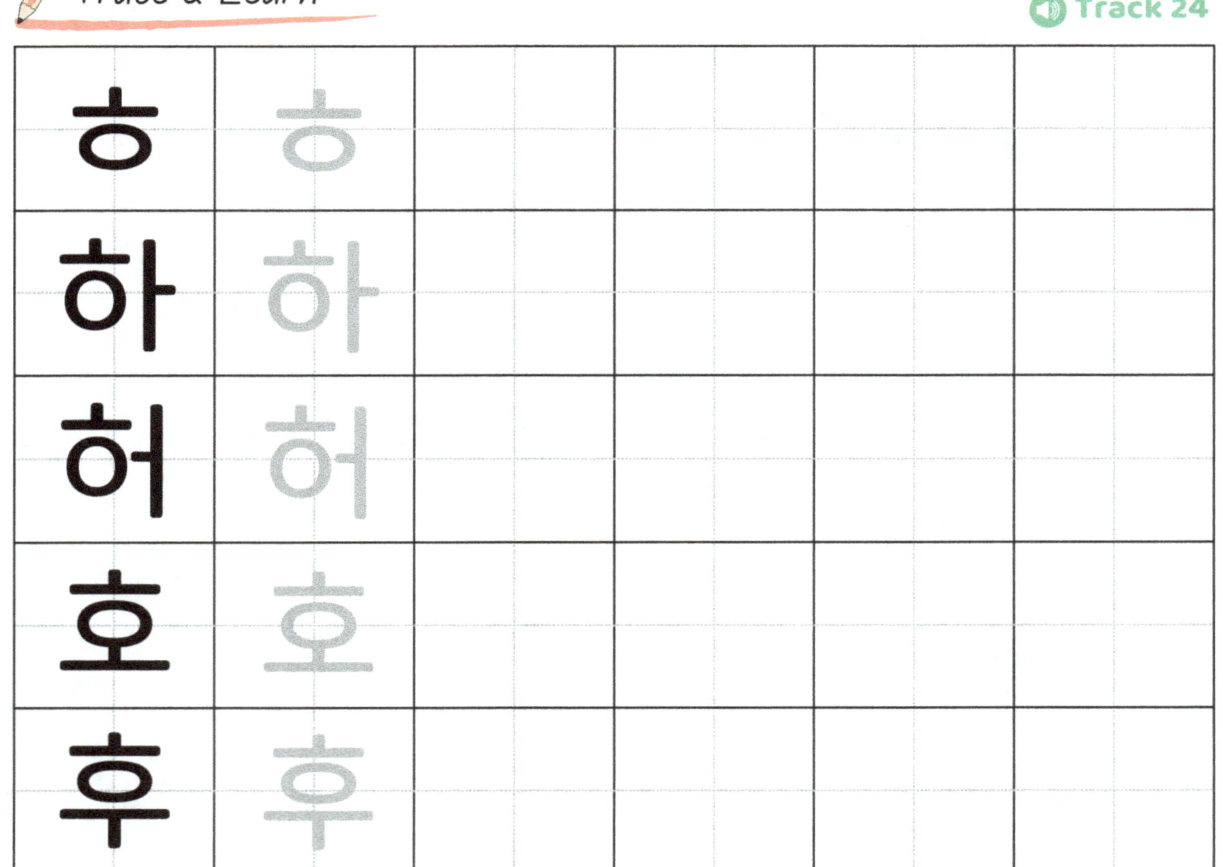

Example

하 허 호 후 흐 히 좋 읗

✏️ *Trace & Learn*

🔊 **Track 24**

1

Hippo

하 마

2

Walnut

호 두

3

Black pepper

후 추

다음 글자를 써보세요.
Practice writing the letters below.

ㄱ	/g/ /k/	ㄱ	ㄱ			
ㄴ	/n/	ㄴ	ㄴ			
ㄷ	/d/ /t/	ㄷ	ㄷ			
ㄹ	/r/ /l/	ㄹ	ㄹ			
ㅁ	/m/	ㅁ	ㅁ			
ㅂ	/b/ /p/	ㅂ	ㅂ			
ㅅ	/s/	ㅅ	ㅅ			
ㅇ	silent	ㅇ	ㅇ			
ㅈ	/tʃ/	ㅈ	ㅈ			
ㅊ	/tʃʰ/	ㅊ	ㅊ			
ㅋ	/kʰ/	ㅋ	ㅋ			
ㅌ	/tʰ/	ㅌ	ㅌ			
ㅍ	/pʰ/	ㅍ	ㅍ			
ㅎ	/h/	ㅎ	ㅎ			

	ㅏ	ㅓ	ㅗ	ㅜ	ㅡ	ㅣ	ㅐ	ㅔ
ㄱ	가							
ㄴ		너						
ㄷ			도					
ㄹ				루				
ㅁ					으			
ㅂ						비		
ㅅ							새	
ㅇ								에
ㅈ								
ㅊ								
ㅋ								
ㅌ								
ㅍ								
ㅎ								

1. 다음 글자를 잘 듣고 소리 내어 읽어보세요.

Listen carefully and read out loud the following letters.

| 1 고 | 2 너 | 3 드 | 4 리 | 5 채 |
| 6 비 | 7 수 | 8 제 | 9 포 | 10 타 |

2. 다음을 잘 듣고 맞으면 O표, 틀리면 X표를 하세요.

Listen carefully and mark O for correct or X for incorrect.

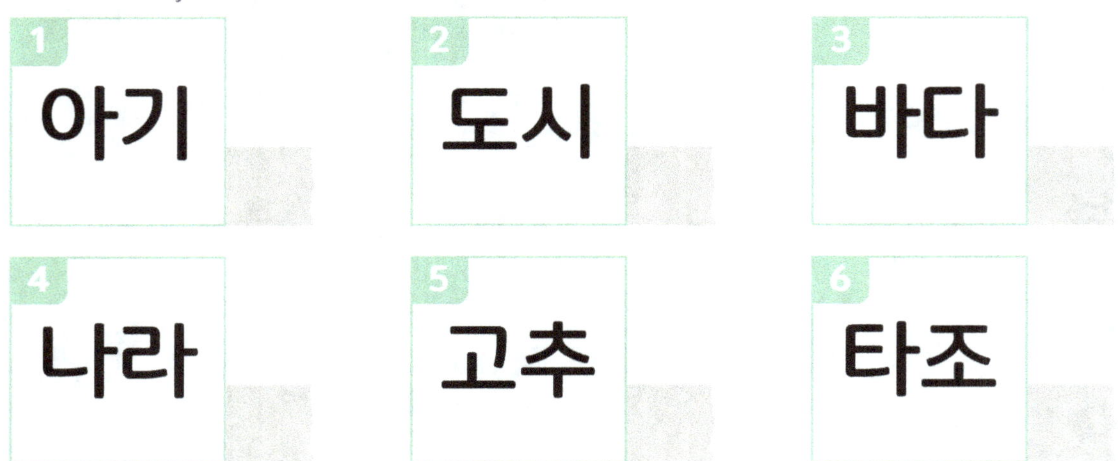

| 1 아기 | 2 도시 | 3 바다 |
| 4 나라 | 5 고추 | 6 타조 |

3. 잘 듣고 맞는 글자에 O표 하세요.

Listen carefully and mark O on the correct letter.

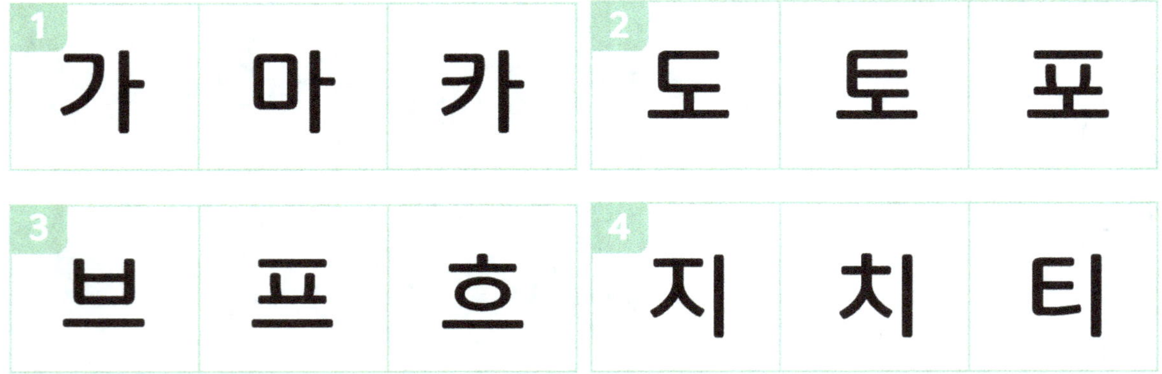

| 1 가 마 카 | 2 도 토 포 |
| 3 브 프 흐 | 4 지 치 티 |

4. 잘 듣고 단어를 받아쓰세요.

Listen carefully and dictate the word.

5. 다음 그림에 알맞은 단어를 쓰세요.

Write the matched word under the picture.

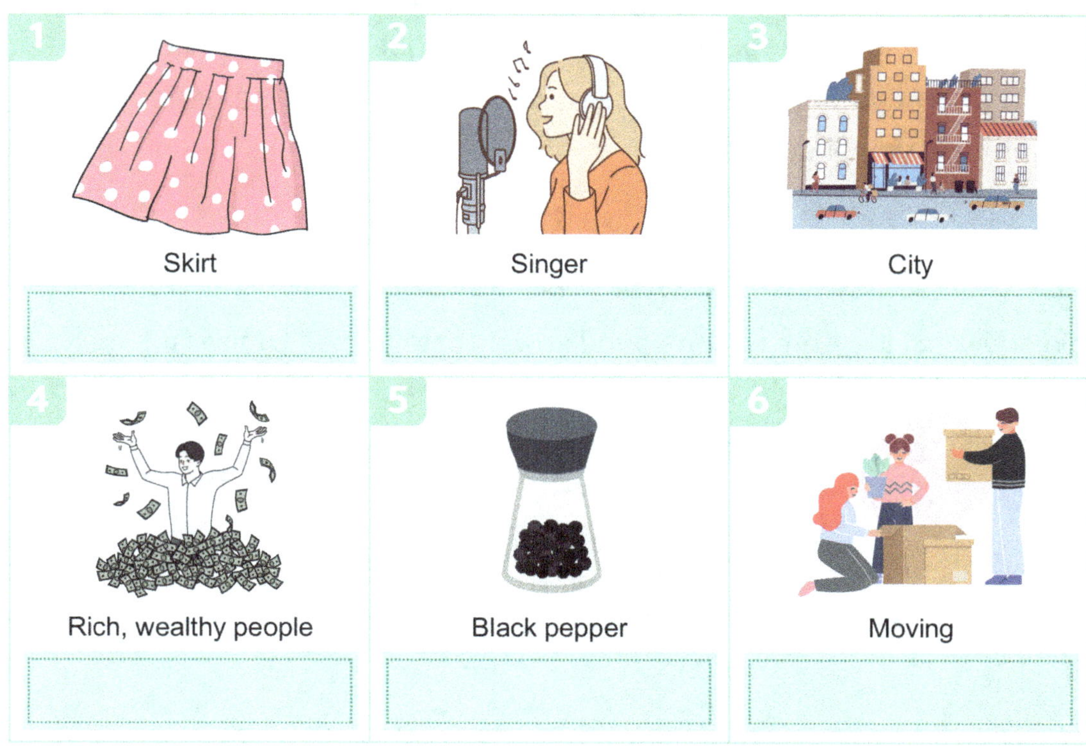

2. (1) O (2) O (3) X [파다] (4) O (5) X [고주] (6) X [다조]
3. (1) 카 (2) 도 (3) 프 (4) 지
4. (1) 가구 (2) 머리 (3) 지구 (4) 포도
5. (1) 치마 (2) 가수 (3) 도시 (4) 부자 (5) 후추 (6) 이사

3. Compound Vowel

이중모음

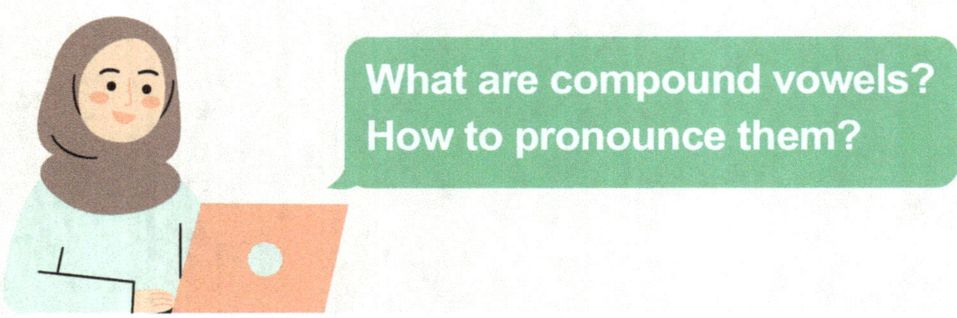

Korean compound vowels are the combination of two single vowels as a result they are pronounced the combining two vowel sounds.

To pronounce them correctly, make the first vowel sound shorter and the second vowel sound longer. Do not pronounce them as two separate vowels quickly or keep the same length for both vowel sounds.

Korean compound vowels   *Pronunciation: /IPA/*

This table shows all the Korean compound vowels categorized by the first sound.

First Vowel Sound	ㅣ /i/ /iː/						ㅗ /o/			ㅜ /u/ /ʊ/			ㅡ /ɯ/
	+						+			+			+
Second Vowel Sound	ㅏ /a/	ㅓ /ʌ/ /ə/	ㅗ /o/	ㅜ /u/ /ʊ/	ㅐ /ɛ/	ㅔ /æ/ /e/	ㅏ /a/	ㅣ /i/ /iː/	ㅐ /ɛ/	ㅔ /æ/ /e/	ㅓ /ʌ/ /ə/	ㅣ /i/ /iː/	ㅣ /i/ /iː/
	=						=			=			=
Compound Vowel	ㅑ /ja/	ㅕ /jʌ/	ㅛ /jo/	ㅠ /ju/	ㅒ /jɛ/	ㅖ /je/	ㅘ /wa/	ㅚ ① /we/	ㅙ /wɛ/	ㅞ /we/	ㅝ /wʌ/	ㅟ ① /wi/	ㅢ /ɨi/

① Exception

Unlike other compound vowels, these two vowels do not follow the rule above. To learn the reason behind it, refer to page 20.

How to write them properly?

When writing compound vowels combined with '⊥' or 'ㅜ', be conscious of the rule to maintain the square shape of each syllable.

1. In the case of combining with '⊥', the other vowel's short stroke ' · ' should be placed above '⊥'.
2. In the case of combining with 'ㅜ', the other vowel's short stroke ' · ' should be placed under that.

I feel like some vowels are pronounced the same.

Yes, you are right. Even native speakers can NOT distinguish some vowels' pronunciation. Thus, you can pronounce certain different vowels in the same way.

1	애 /ɛ/	에 /æ//e/	
2	얘 /jɛ/	예 /je/	
3	외 /we/	왜 /wɛ/	웨 /we/

Then why don't Koreans choose just one vowel for a sound?

Each vowel's pronunciation was distinct in the past, but it has been simplified over time. However, as spelling typically tends to change slower than pronunciation, differently written but sounding the same vowels have survived. This tendency can be seen in every other language, even in English. For example, it is a similar idea of homophones in English, write[raɪt] and right[raɪt]. Similar concept is shared in many languages including Korean and by using different spellings it helps to deliver exact meaning in writing without confusion.

Pronunciation	Tip for pronunciation	
IPA /jɑ/ Romanization [ya]	"ya" as in "**ya**cht /jɑːt/" or "**ya**rd /jɑːrd/"	

Stroke order	Font variations	Letter creating principal
	야 야 야	ㆍ + ㅏ

ㅑ
야
[ya]

Example

야 갸 냐 댜 랴 먀 뱍 샷

✏️ *Trace & Learn*

🔊 **Track 26**

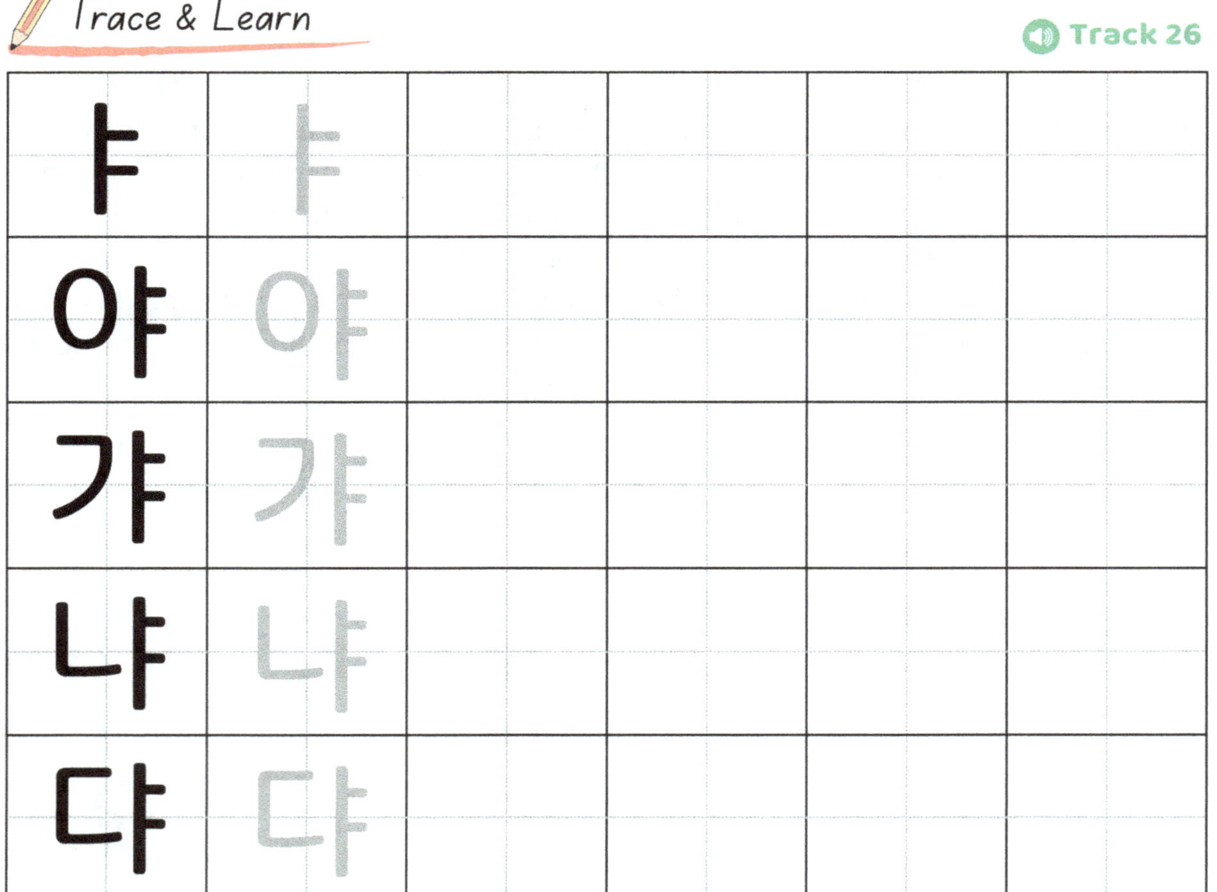

1

Baseball

야	구	야	구

2

Beast

야	수	야	수

3

Coconut palm

야	자	야	자

Pronunciation		Tip for pronunciation
IPA /jʌ/ Romanization [yeo]		"yu" as in "**yu**m /jʌm/"

Stroke order	Font variations	Letter creating principal
	여 여 여	· + ㅓ

ㅕ
여
[yeo]

Example

여 겨 녀 뎌 려 며 볏 형

✏️ Trace & Learn

🔊 Track 27

ㅕ	ㅕ				
여	여				
겨	겨				
녀	녀				
뎌	뎌				

1

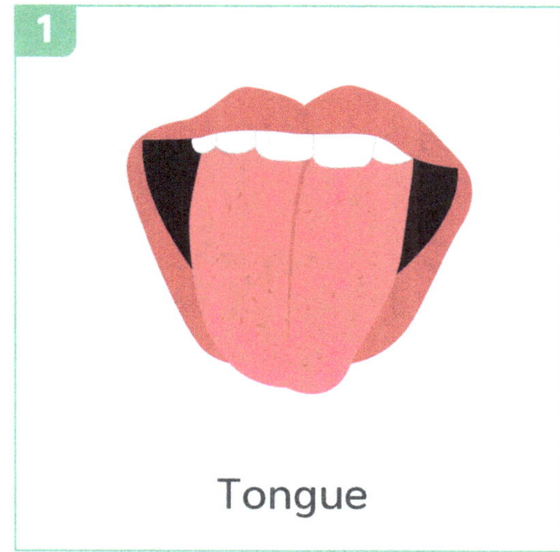

Tongue

혀 혀

2

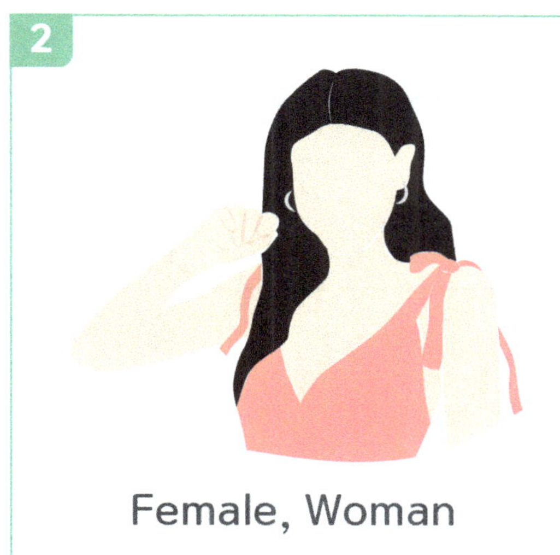

Female, Woman

여 자　여 자

3

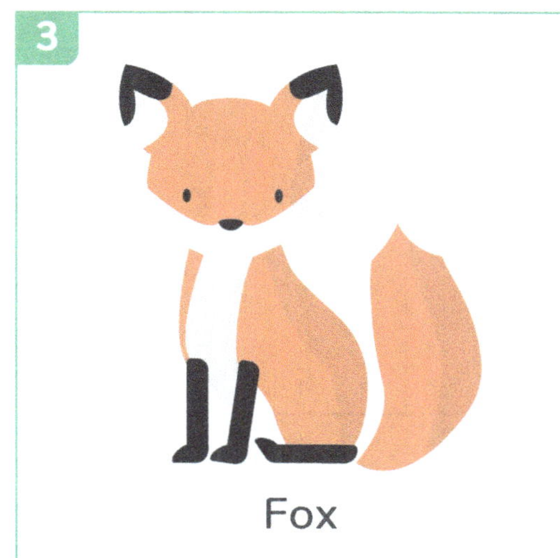

Fox

여 우　여 우

Pronunciation	Tip for pronunciation
IPA /jo/ *Romanization* [yo]	"yo" as in "**yo**ga /joga/"

Stroke order	Font variations	Letter creating principal
	ㅛ ㅛ ㄴ	· ┼ ㅗ

ㅛ
[yo]

Example

요 교 뇨 됴 료 묘 뵨 용

✏️ Trace & Learn

🔊 Track 28

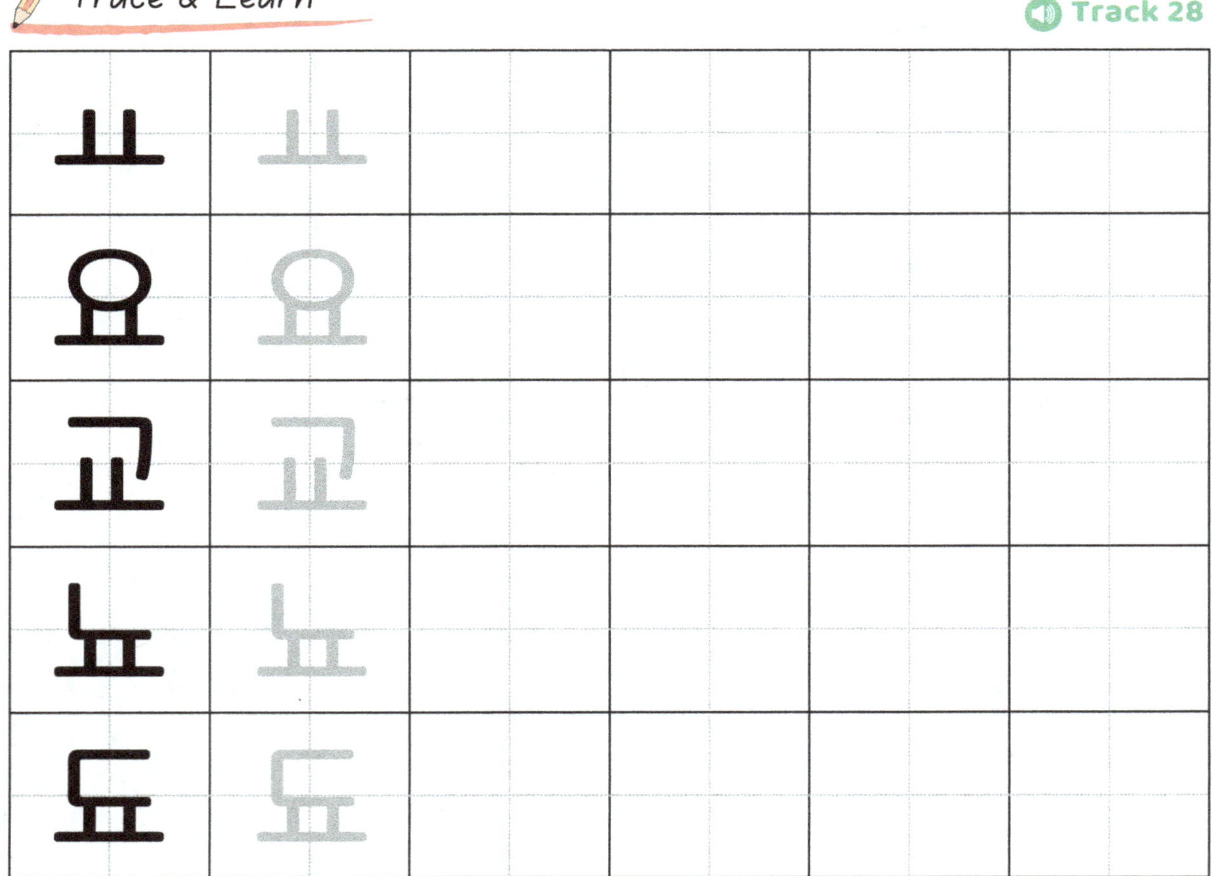

1

Yo-yo

요 요 요 요

2

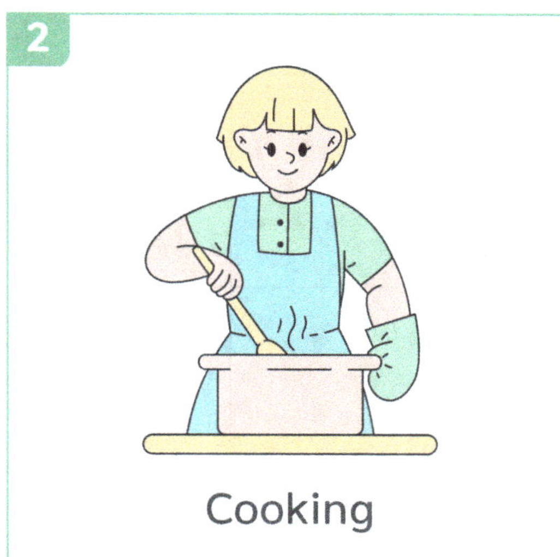

Cooking

요 리 요 리

3

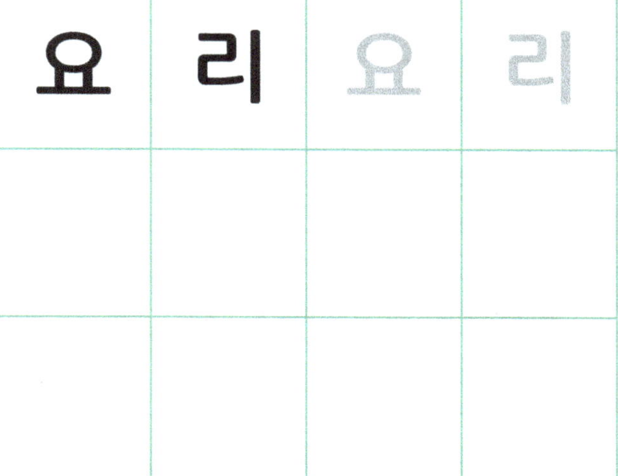

Yoga

요 가 요 가

	Pronunciation	Tip for pronunciation
ㅠ 유 [yu]	IPA /ju/ Romanization [yu]	"u" as in "**U**SA /juː es ˈeɪ/"

Stroke order	Font variations	Letter creating principal
	유 유 유	· ㅓ ㅜ

Example

유 규 뉴 듀 류 뮤 튜 휴

✏️ Trace & Learn

🔊 **Track 29**

ㅠ	ㅠ				
유	유				
규	규				
뉴	뉴				
듀	듀				

1

Milk

우 유 우 유

2

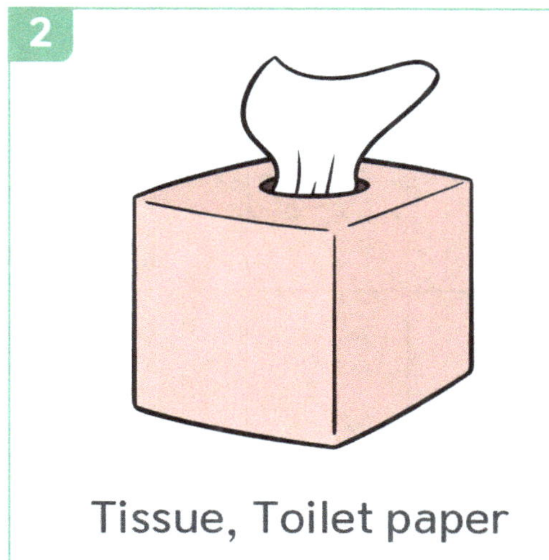
Tissue, Toilet paper

휴 지 휴 지

3

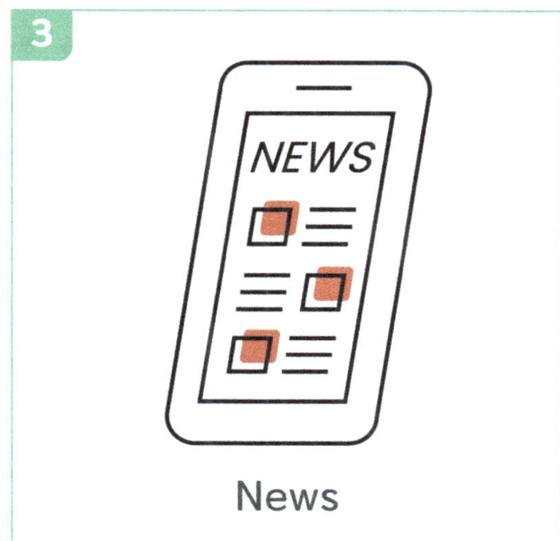
News

뉴 스 뉴 스

ㅒ
얘
[yae]

Pronunciation	Tip for pronunciation
IPA /jɛ/ Romanization [yae]	"ye" as in "**ye**s /jes/" or "**ye**sterday /ˈjes.tɚ.deɪ/" This vowel ㅒ and the vowel ㅖ sound similar. Many Koreans cannot distinguish the difference in pronunciation between the two.

Stroke order	Font variations	Letter creating principal
ㅒ	얘 얘 얘	· + ㅐ

Example

얘 걔 먜 쟤 섀 얜 걘 쟨

Trace & Learn

Track 30

ㅒ	ㅒ			
얘	얘			
걔	걔			
냬	냬			
댸	댸			

1

He or She (near you)
Casual tone

얘 · 얘

2

He or She (not in here)
Casual tone

개 · 개

3

Story
(It's short for 이야기)

얘 기 · 얘 기

 ㅖ (' ㅣ ' + Vowel)

Pronunciation		Tip for pronunciation
IPA	/je/	"ye" as in "**ye**s /jes/" or "**ye**sterday /ˈjes.tɚ.deɪ/" The previous vowel ㅒ and this vowel ㅖ sound similar. Many Koreans cannot distinguish the difference in pronunciation between the two.
Romanization	[ye]	

Stroke order	Font variations	Letter creating principal
	예 예 예	· + ㅖ

ㅖ
예
[ye]

Example

예 계 녜 뎨 례 메 옌 현

Trace & Learn

Track 31

1

Worship

예 배

2

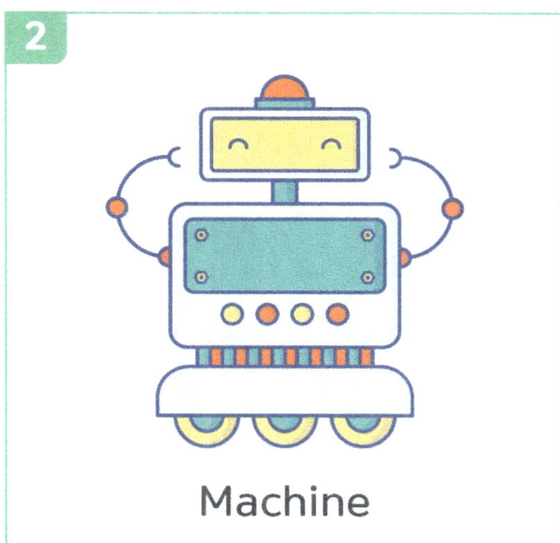

Machine

기 계

3

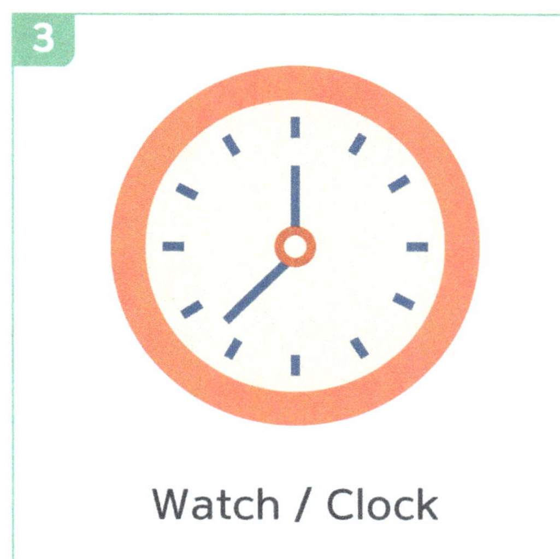

Watch / Clock

시 계

다음 글자를 써보세요.
Practice writing the letters below.

ㅑ	/ja/	ㅑ	ㅑ			
ㅕ	/jʌ/	ㅕ	ㅕ			
ㅛ	/jo/	ㅛ	ㅛ			
ㅠ	/ju/	ㅠ	ㅠ			
ㅒ	/jɛ/	ㅒ	ㅒ			
ㅖ	/je/	ㅖ	ㅖ			
야	야					
여	여					
요	요					
유	유					
애	애					
예	예					

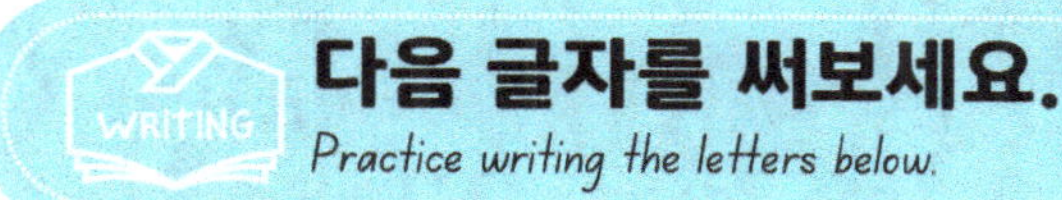

다음 글자를 써보세요.

Practice writing the letters below.

	ㅑ	ㅕ	ㅛ	ㅠ	ㅒ	ㅖ
ㄱ	갸					
ㄴ		녀				
ㄷ			됴			
ㄹ				류		
ㅁ					먜	
ㅂ						볘
ㅅ						
ㅇ						
ㅈ						
ㅊ						
ㅋ						
ㅌ						
ㅍ						
ㅎ						

연습 문제
Practice

Track 32

1. 다음 글자를 잘 듣고 소리 내어 읽어보세요.
   Listen carefully and read out loud the following letters.

2. 다음을 잘 듣고 맞으면 O표, 틀리면 X표를 하세요.
   Listen carefully and mark O for correct or X for incorrect.

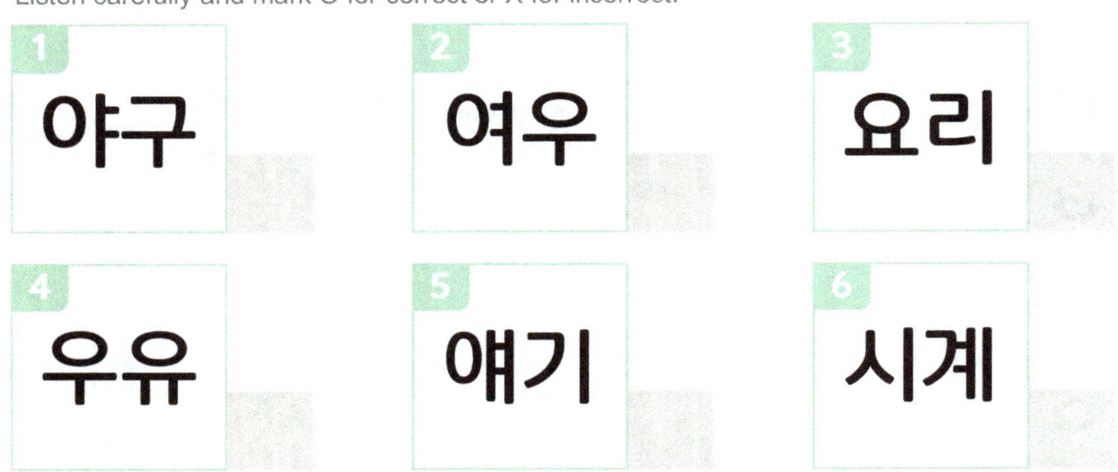

3. 잘 듣고 맞는 글자에 O표 하세요.
   Listen carefully and mark O on the correct letter.

4. 잘 듣고 단어를 받아쓰세요.

Listen carefully and dictate the word.

<table>
<tr><td>1</td><td></td></tr>
<tr><td>2</td><td></td></tr>
<tr><td>3</td><td></td></tr>
<tr><td>4</td><td></td></tr>
</table>

5. 다음 그림에 알맞은 단어를 쓰세요.

Write the matched word under the picture.

1	2	3
Tongue	Clock / Watch	Baseball
4	5	6
Milk	Story (It's short for 이야기)	Cooking

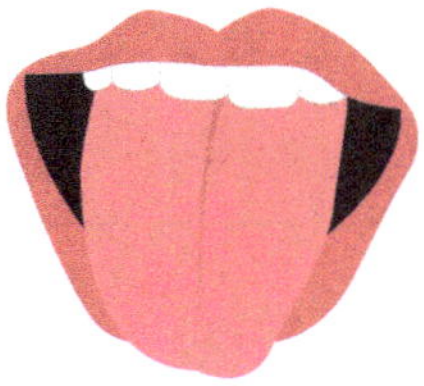

A

2. (1) O (2) X [야유] (3) X [유리] (4) O (5) X [애기/에기] (6) O
3. (1) 여 (2) 규 (3) 쟤 (4) 셔
4. (1) 여자 (2) 휴지 (3) 기계 (4) 야자
5. (1) 혀 (2) 시계 (3) 야구 (4) 우유 (5) 얘기 (6) 요리

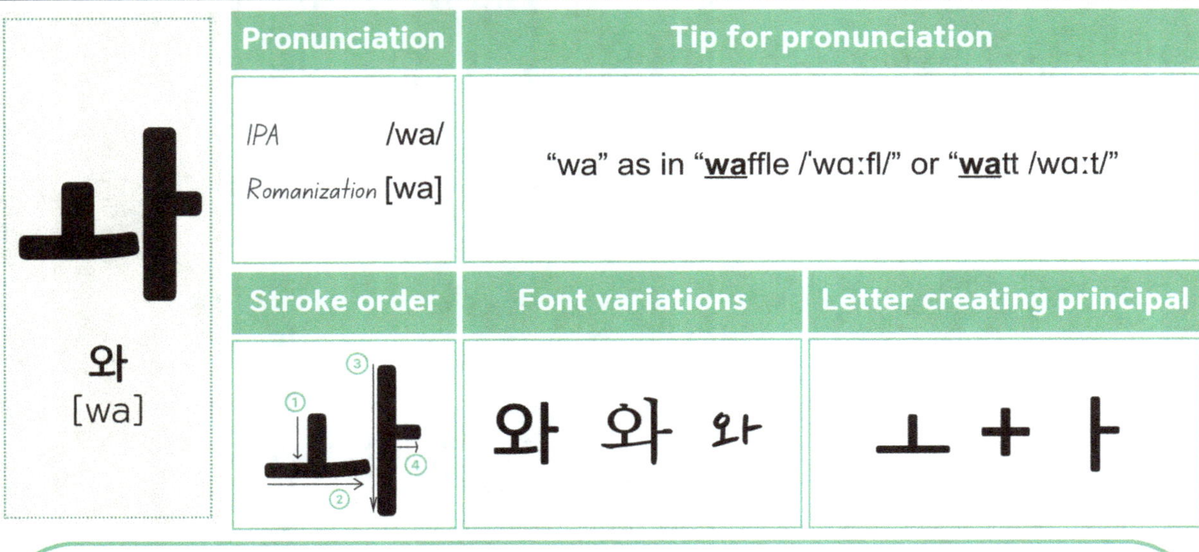

Pronunciation	Tip for pronunciation	
IPA　　　/wa/ Romanization [wa]	"wa" as in "**wa**ffle /ˈwɑːfl/" or "**wa**tt /wɑːt/"	

Stroke order	Font variations	Letter creating principal
	와 와 와	ㅗ + ㅏ

Example

와 과 놔 돠 롸 뫄 관 촬

✏️ *Trace & Learn*　　　　🔊 **Track 33**

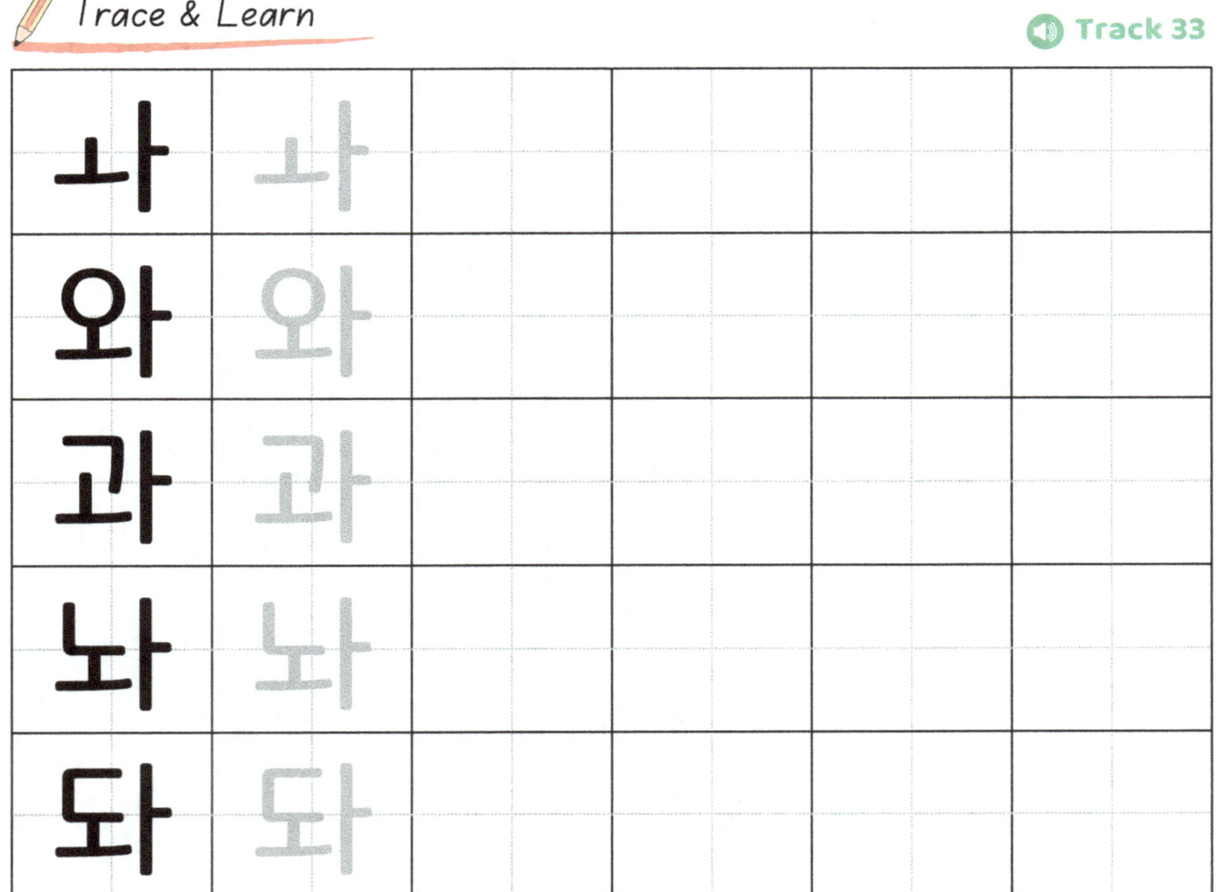

1

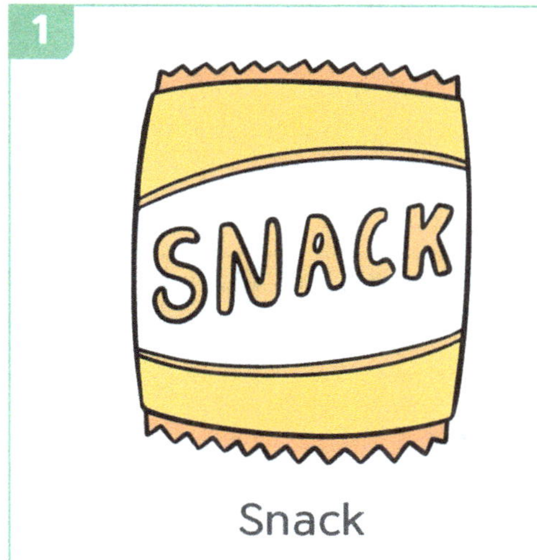

Snack

과 자 　과 　자

2

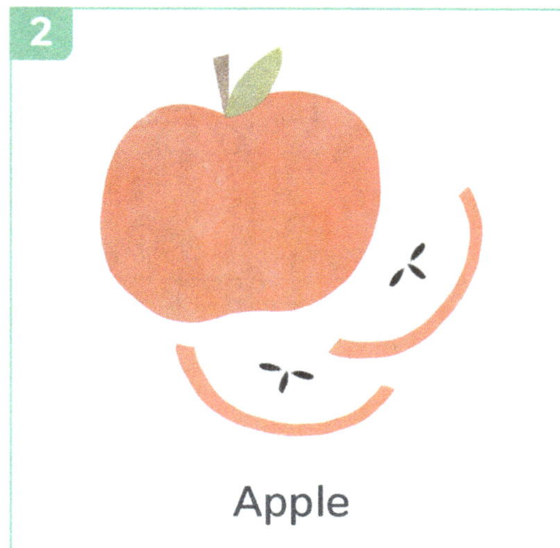

Apple

사 과 　사 　과

3

Painter

화 가 　화 　가

Pronunciation	Tip for pronunciation
IPA /we/ Romanization [oe]	"we" as in "**we**ll /wɛl/" or "**we**st /wɛst/" The vowels ㅔ, ㅐ and this vowel ㅚ sound similar. Many Koreans cannot distinguish the difference in pronunciation between them.

ㅚ

외
[oe]

Stroke order	Font variations	Letter creating principal
	외 외 외	ㅗ + ㅣ

Example

외 괴 뇌 되 룈 뮌 뷘 쇨

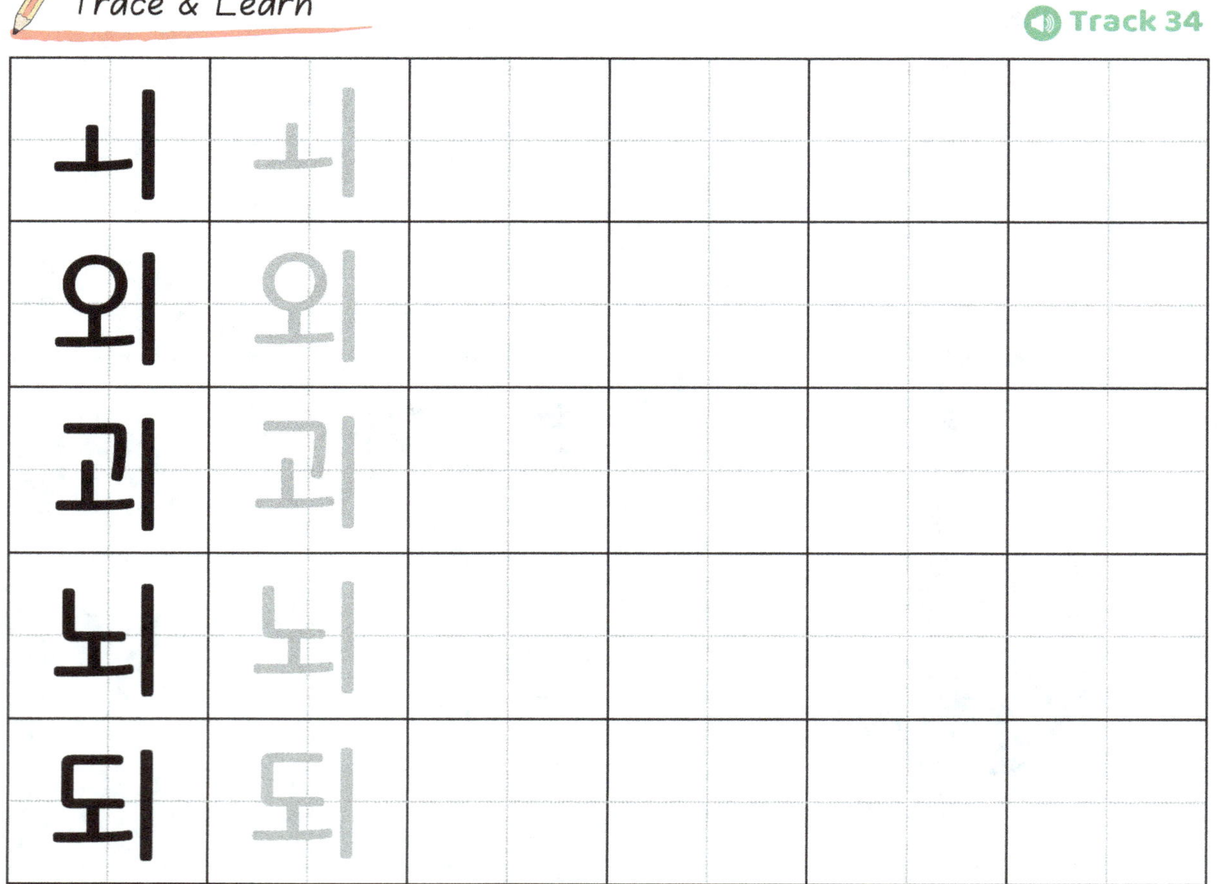

✏️ Trace & Learn

🔊 Track 34

ㅚ	ㅚ				
외	외				
괴	괴				
뇌	뇌				
되	되				

1

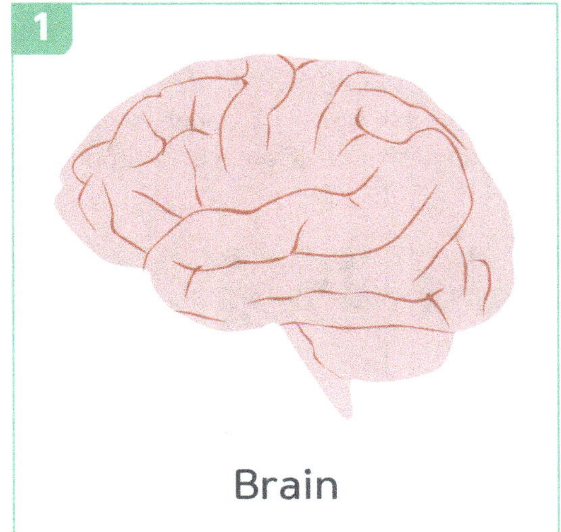

Brain

뇌 뇌

2

Company

회 사 회 사

3

Church

교 회 교 회

ㅙ

왜
[wae]

Pronunciation	Tip for pronunciation
IPA /wɛ/ Romanization [wae]	"we" as in "**we**ll /wɛl/" or "**we**st /wɛst/" The vowels ㅚ, ㅞ and this vowel ㅙ sound similar. Many Koreans cannot distinguish the difference in pronunciation between them.

Stroke order	Font variations	Letter creating principal
ㅙ	왜 왜 왜	ㅗ + ㅐ

Example

왜 괘 돼 좌 봬 쾌 괭 횟

Trace & Learn

Track 35

1

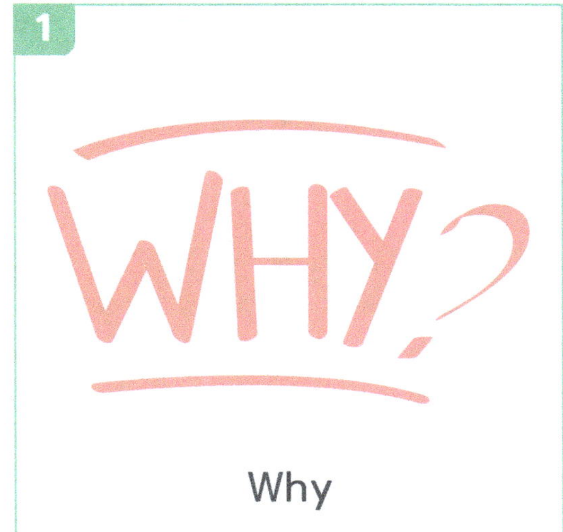

Why

| 왜 | 왜 | | |

2

Pig

| 돼 | 지 | 돼 | 지 |

3

To be cheerful / delightful

| 유 | 쾌 | 하 | 다 |
| 유 | 쾌 | 하 | 다 |

Pronunciation		Tip for pronunciation
IPA	/we/	"we" as in "**we**ll /wel/" or "**we**st /west/"
Romanization	[we]	The previous vowels ㅚ, ㅙ and this vowel ㅞ sound similar. Many Koreans cannot distinguish the difference in pronunciation between them.

뒈
웨
[we]

Stroke order	Font variations	Letter creating principal
	웨 웨 웨	ㅜ + ㅔ

Example

웨 궤 눼 뒈 뤠 뭬 쉥 휑

✏️ *Trace & Learn*

🔊 **Track 36**

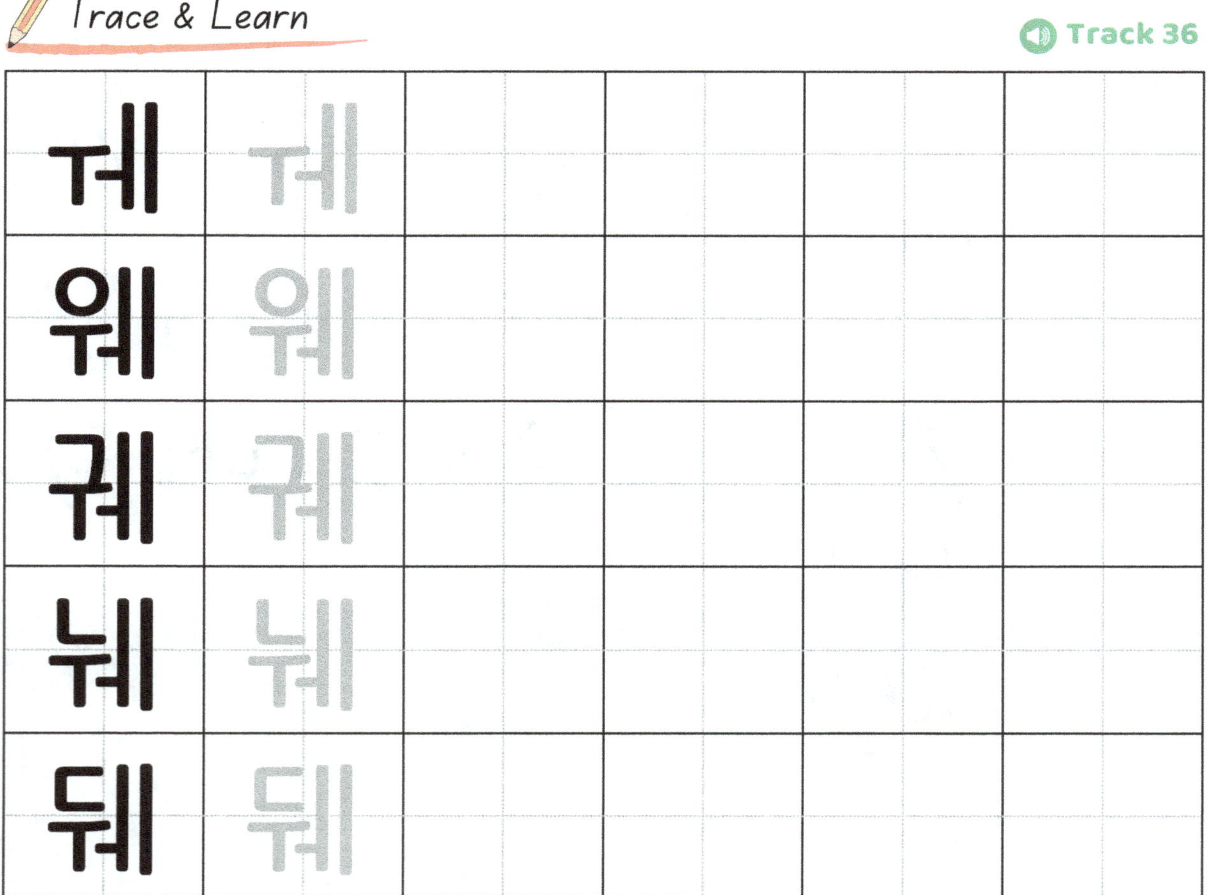

1

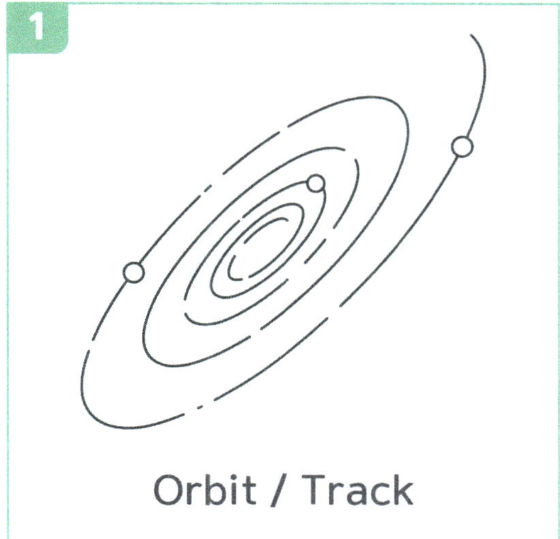

Orbit / Track

궤	도	궤	도

2

Sweater

스	웨	터
스	웨	터

3

Waiter

웨	이	터
웨	이	터

	워 [wo]

Pronunciation	Tip for pronunciation
IPA /wʌ/ Romanization [wo]	"wo" as in "**wo**nder /ˈwʌndə(r)/"

Stroke order	Font variations	Letter creating principal
	워 워 워	ㅜ + ㅓ

Example

워 궈 눠 둬 뤄 뭐 원 훨

✏️ Trace & Learn

🔊 **Track 37**

워	워				
워	워				
궈	궈				
눠	눠				
둬	둬				

1

What

뭐	뭐		

2

(weather) Hot
Casual tone

더	워	더	워

3

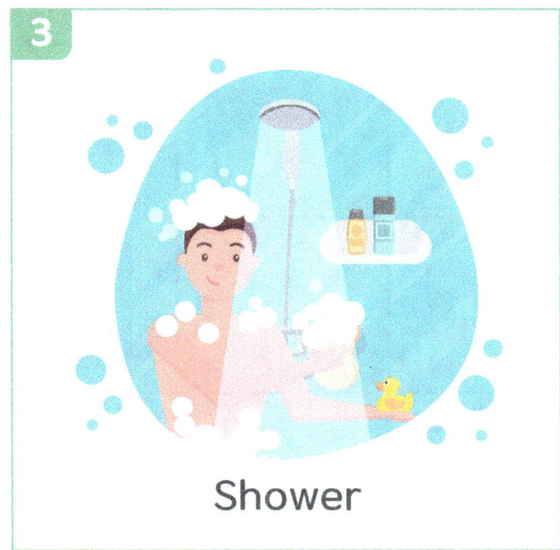

Shower

샤	워	샤	워

Pronunciation	Tip for pronunciation
IPA /wi/ Romanization [wi]	"we" as in "**we** /wi/"

Stroke order	Font variations	Letter creating principal
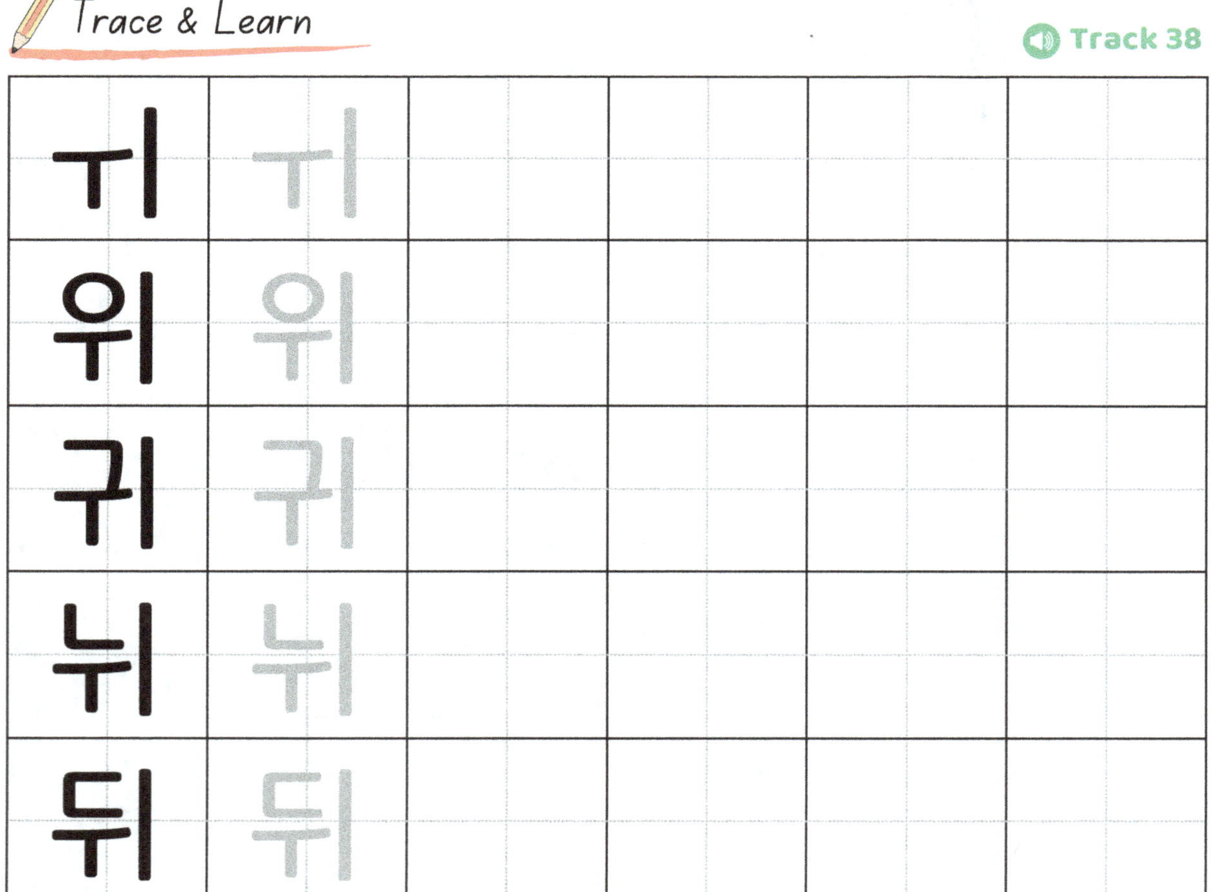	위 위 위	ㅜ + ㅣ

ㅟ
위
[wi]

Example

위 귀 뉘 뒤 륄 뮐 뷘 쉼

✏️ Trace & Learn

🔊 Track 38

ㅟ	ㅟ				
위	위				
귀	귀				
뉘	뉘				
뒤	뒤				

1

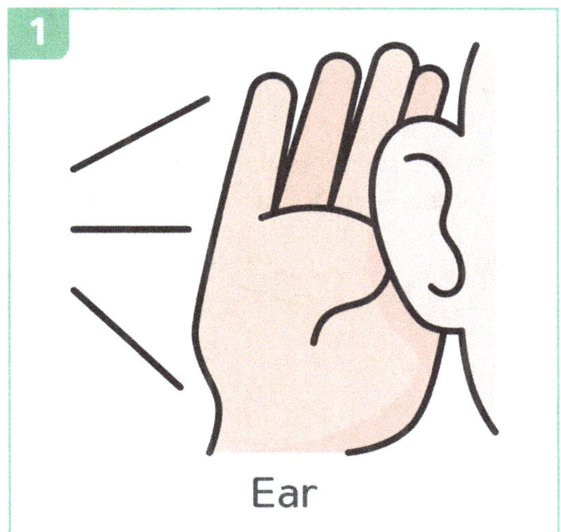

Ear

귀	귀		

2

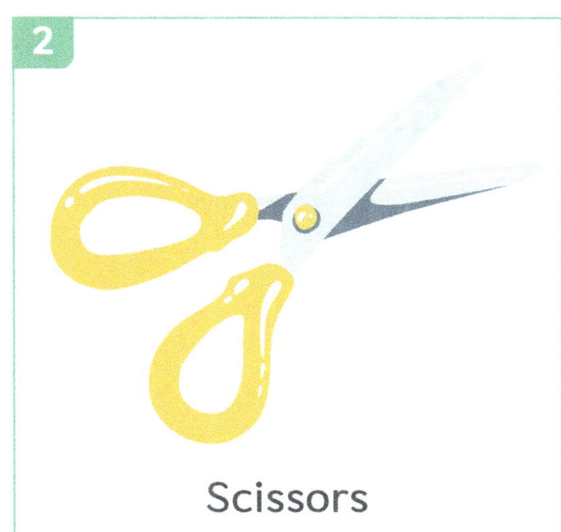

Scissors

가	위	가	위

3

Wheel

바	퀴	바	퀴

Pronunciation	Tip for pronunciation
IPA /ɰi/ Romanization [ui]	This vowel is not found in English. Pronounce the 'ㅡ' short and the 'ㅣ' longer. It is not easy to pronounce the 'ㅢ', so the pronunciation change depends on the position of the words. (Refer to Pages 164-165)

ㅢ
의
[ui]

Stroke order	Font variations	Letter creating principal
① → ㅢ ②	의 의 의	ㅡ + ㅣ

Example

의 긔 늬 희 읜 닌 신 핀

Trace & Learn

Track 39

1

Chair

의 자　의 자

2

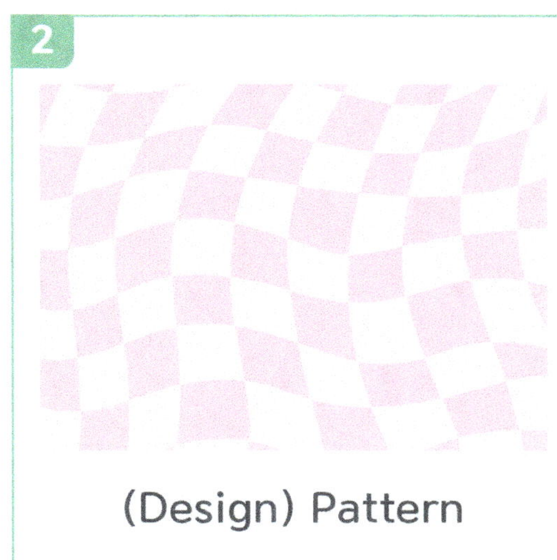

(Design) Pattern

무 늬　무 늬

3

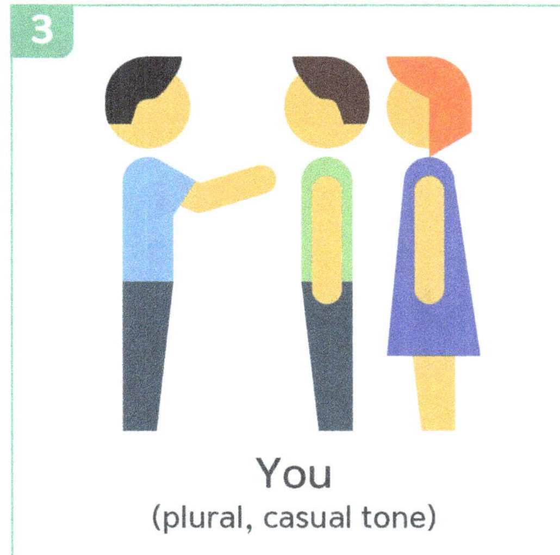

You
(plural, casual tone)

너 희　너 희

다음 글자를 써보세요.
Practice writing the letters below.

과	/wa/	과	과			
긔	/we/	긔	긔			
괘	/wɛ/	괘	괘			
궤	/we/	궤	궤			
궈	/wʌ/	궈	궈			
귀	/wi/	귀	귀			
긔	/ɰi/	긔	긔			
와	와					
외	외					
왜	왜					
웨	웨					
워	워					
위	위					
의	의					

	ㅘ	ㅚ	ㅙ	ㅖ	ㅕ	ㅟ	ㅢ
ㄱ	과						
ㄴ		뇌					
ㄷ			돼				
ㄹ				뤠			
ㅁ					워		
ㅂ						뷔	
ㅅ							싀
ㅇ							
ㅈ							
ㅊ							
ㅋ							
ㅌ							
ㅍ							
ㅎ							

1. 다음 글자를 잘 듣고 소리 내어 읽어보세요.
Listen carefully and read out loud the following letters.

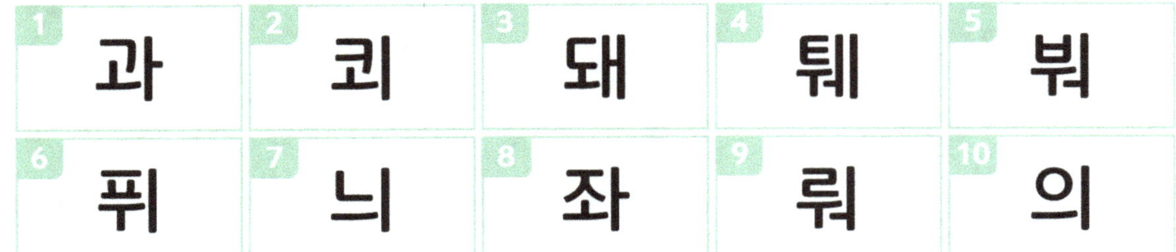

| 1 과 | 2 쾨 | 3 돼 | 4 퉤 | 5 붜 |
| 6 퓌 | 7 늬 | 8 좌 | 9 뤄 | 10 의 |

2. 다음을 잘 듣고 맞으면 O표, 틀리면 X표를 하세요.
Listen carefully and mark O for correct or X for incorrect.

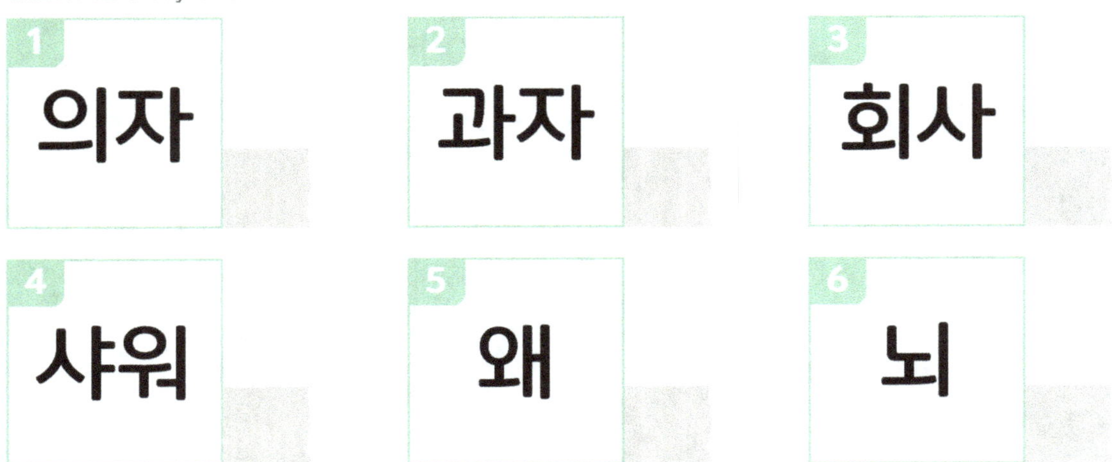

| 1 의자 | 2 과자 | 3 회사 |
| 4 샤워 | 5 왜 | 6 뇌 |

3. 잘 듣고 맞는 글자에 O표 하세요.
Listen carefully and mark O on the correct letter.

| 1 예 왜 위 | 2 의 으 이 |
| 3 위 외 의 | 4 왜 애 얘 |

4. 잘 듣고 단어를 받아쓰세요.

Listen carefully and dictate the word.

5. 다음 그림에 알맞은 단어를 쓰세요.

Write the matched word under the picture.

4. Double Consonant

쌍자음

These consonants (ㄱ, ㄷ, ㅅ, ㅂ, ㅈ) can become double consonants by doubling themselves (ㄲ, ㄸ, ㅆ, ㅃ, ㅉ).
Pronounce double consonants with strained vocal sounds. These consonants **are pronounced with a higher pitch and more tensing sound**. Unfortunately, there is no equivalent pronunciation in English. So listen to the audio carefully and practice it until you feel comfortable.

Double consonant *Pronunciation: /IPA/

ㄱ	/g/ /k/			ㄲ	/k'/
ㄷ	/d/ /t/			ㄸ	/t'/
ㅂ	/b/ /p/	**+** The same Consonant *This makes a tense sound* **=**		ㅃ	/p'/
ㅅ	/s/			ㅆ	/s'/
ㅈ	/tʃ/ /dʒ/			ㅉ	/tʃ'/

Flat - Aspirated - Tense consonant relationship

You may have noticed some other consonants that sound similar to these. Five consonants exhibit a close association with others, as shown on the next page. Flat consonants are the base sounds and to pronounce aspirated or tense consonants, follow the patterns provided on the next page.

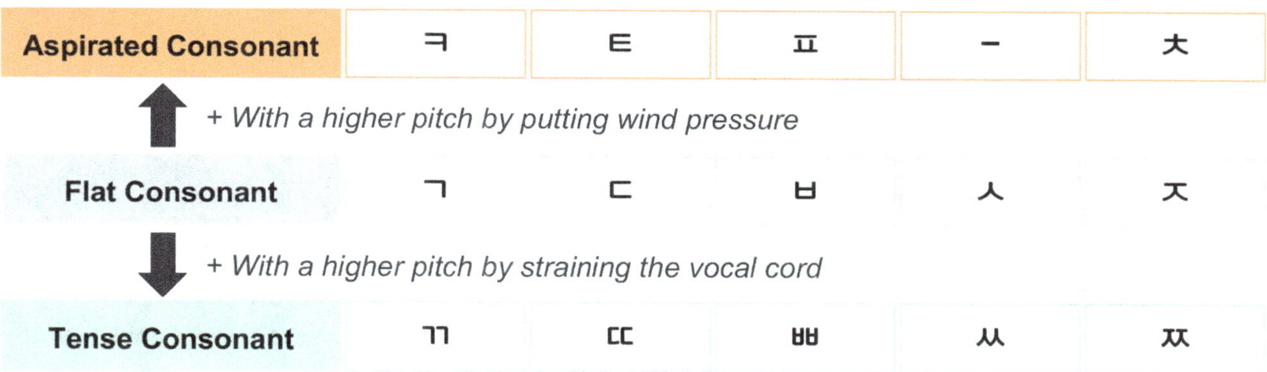

1) How can I articulate them accurately?

- **Use a higher pitch for aspirated and tense consonants.**

  Aspirated and tense consonants are pronounced with higher pitch compared to flat consonants.

- **Add a wind pressure when pronouncing aspirated ones.**

  Aspirated consonants' pronunciations need more air pressure than other types of consonants.

- **Strain your vocal cords to articulate tense consonants.**

  Straining your vocal cords to pronounce tense consonants. Remember the location of the strain area in your vocal cord every time you pronounce tense ones.

2) Is accurate pronunciation important?

- YES. Otherwise, it may cause miscommunication. For example, there are words 자다, 차다, 짜다. As you see here, the only difference is the consonant on the first syllable. But each word's meanings are very different. 자다 is to sleep. 차다 means to kick, and 짜다 means to be salty. So, if you accidentally say the wrong one, it may lead the conversation in the wrong direction.

  - **다음 글자를 소리 내어 읽어보세요.** (Refer to video #4. Double Consonant)
    Read out loud the following words.

ㄲ

쌍기역
[ssang-
gi-yeok]

Pronunciation	Tip for pronunciation
IPA /k'/ Romanization [kk]	To pronounce, strain your vocal cords and use a higher pitch compared to when pronouncing 'ㄱ'. ❗ Your tongue root moves a bit more upward compared to when pronouncing 'ㄱ'.

Stroke order	Font variations
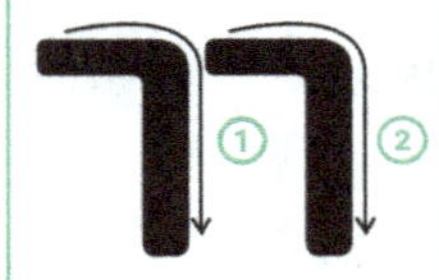	까 까 까 까

Example

까 꺼 꼬 꾸 끄 끼 깬 낄

✏️ *Trace & Learn*

🔊 **Track 41**

ㄲ	ㄲ				
까	까				
꺼	꺼				
꼬	꼬				
꾸	꾸				

1

Sesame seed / Perilla seed

깨 | 깨

2

Rabbit

토 끼 | 토 끼

3

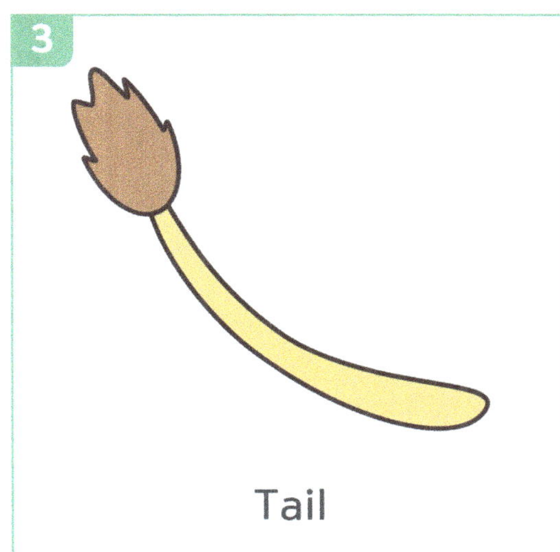

Tail

꼬 리 | 꼬 리

Pronunciation		Tip for pronunciation
IPA	/t'/	To pronounce, strain your vocal cords and use a higher pitch compared to when pronouncing 'ㄷ'.
Romanization	[tt]	❗ Touch the roof of your mouth with your tongue tip, but the area of your tongue tip should be wider.

ㄸ

쌍디귿
[ssang-di-geut]

Stroke order	Font variations
	따 따 따 따

Example

따 떠 또 뚜 뜨 띠 땔 뜀

✏️ *Trace & Learn*

🔊 **Track 42**

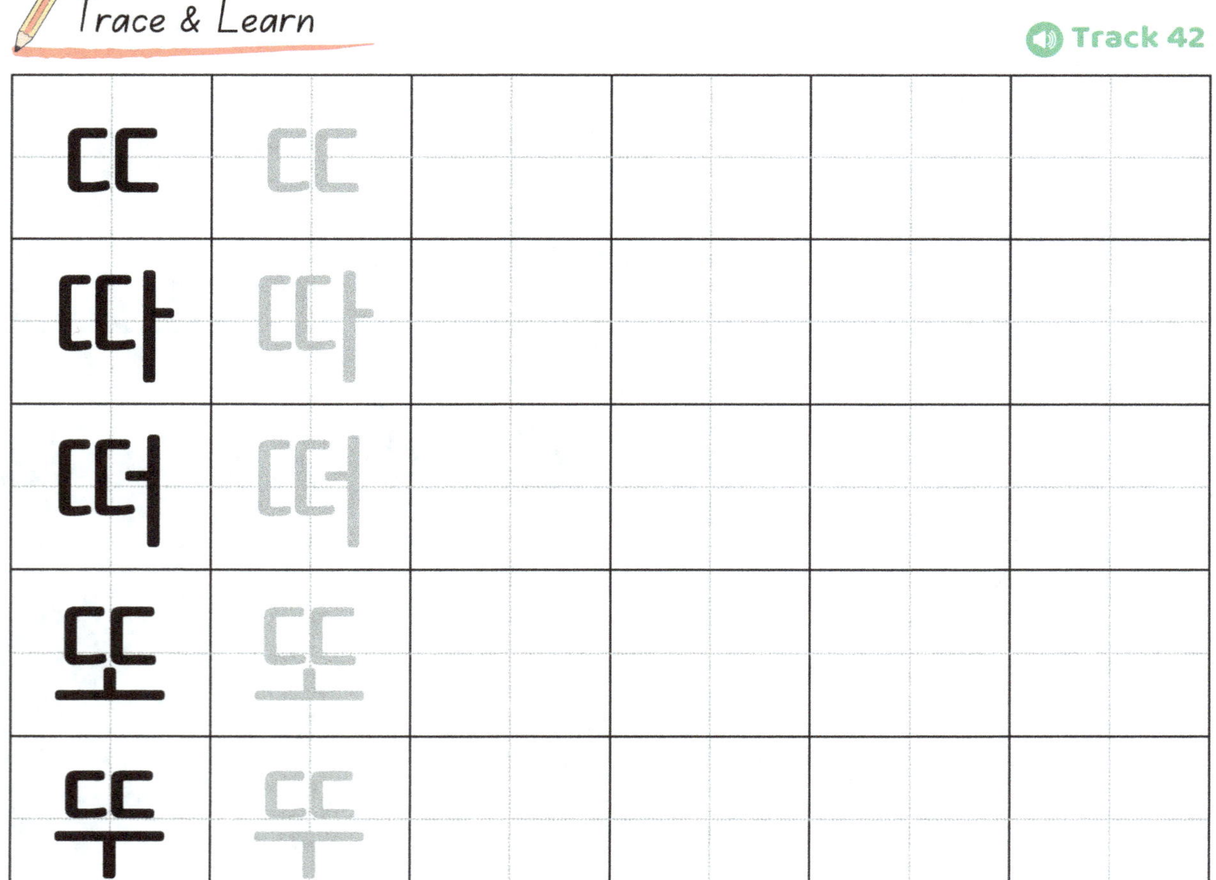

1

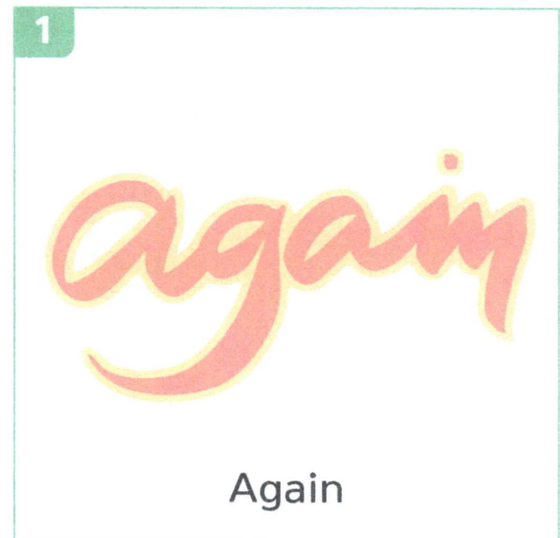

Again

또　또

2

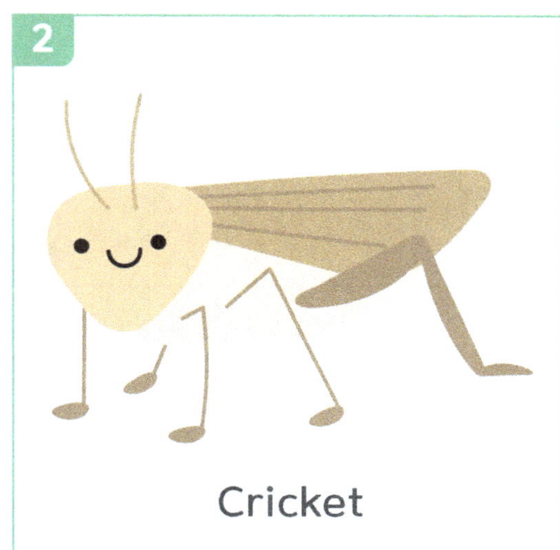

Cricket

귀　뚜　라　미
귀　뚜　라　미

3

Hair band

머　리　띠
머　리　띠

Pronunciation	Tip for pronunciation
IPA /p'/ Romanization [pp]	To pronounce, strain your vocal cords and use a higher pitch compared to when pronouncing 'ㅂ'. ❶ Put more pressure on your lips and throat and make sure both lips touch each other longer than ㅂ.

ㅃ

쌍비읍
[ssang-
bi-eup]

Stroke order	Font variations
	빠　빠　빠　빠

Example

빠　뻐　뽀　뿌　쁘　삐　뺌　뻥

✏️ *Trace & Learn*

🔊 **Track 43**

ㅃ	ㅃ				
빠	빠				
뻐	뻐				
뽀	뽀				
뿌	뿌				

1

Kiss (lightly)

뽀 뽀 뽀 뽀

2

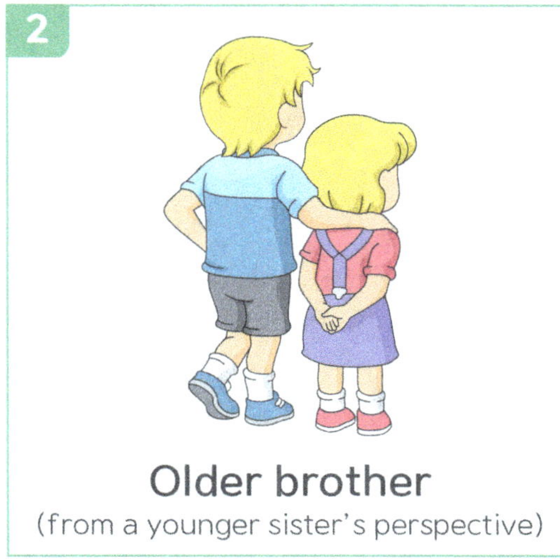

Older brother
(from a younger sister's perspective)

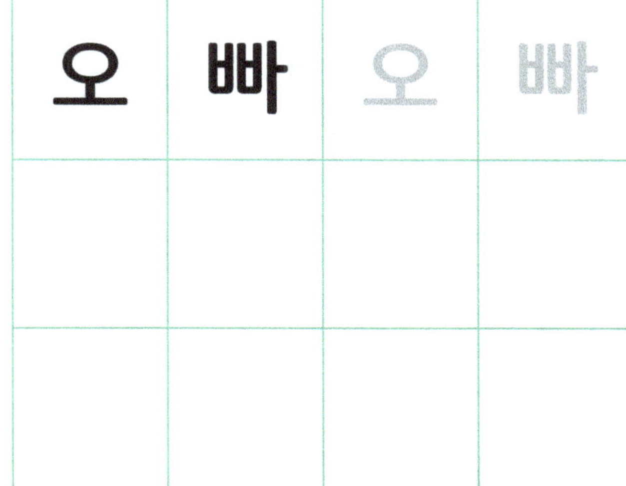

오 빠 오 빠

3

Root

뿌 리 뿌 리

ㅆ

쌍시옷
[ssang-si-ot]

Pronunciation	Tip for pronunciation
IPA /s'/ Romanization [ss]	To pronounce, strain your vocal cords and use a higher pitch compared to when pronouncing 'ㅅ'. ❗ The sound is relatively shorter and stronger than the one of 'ㅅ'.

Stroke order	Font variations
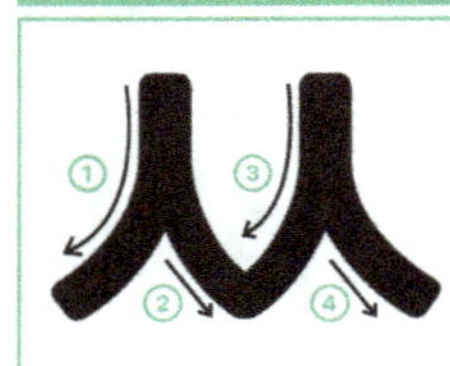	싸 싸 싸 싸

Example

싸 써 쏘 쑤 쓰 씨 쌤 쐰

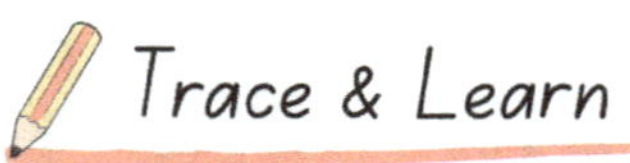

Trace & Learn

🔊 Track 44

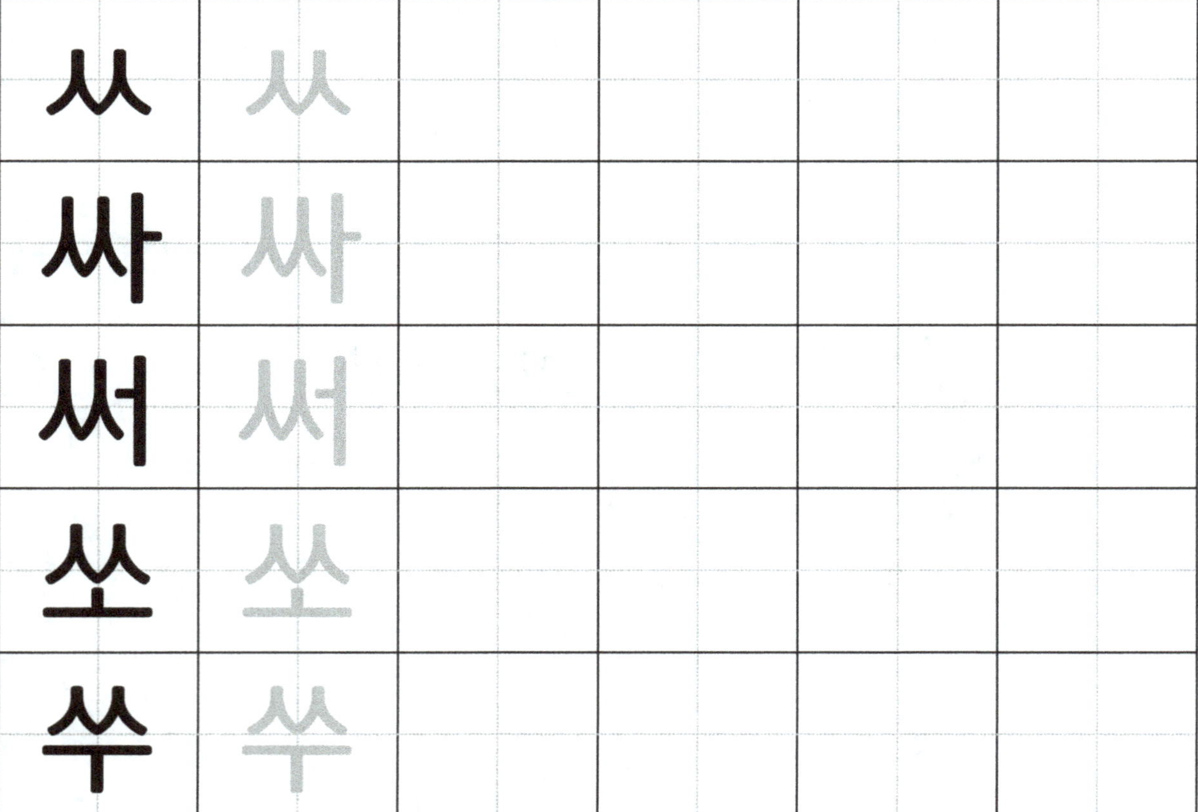

1

Seed

씨 | 씨

2

Middle-aged man

아 | 저 | 씨
아 | 저 | 씨

3

Trash

쓰 | 레 | 기
쓰 | 레 | 기

ㅉ

쌍지읏
[ssang-
ji-eut]

Pronunciation	Tip for pronunciation
IPA /tʃ'/ Romanization [jj]	To pronounce, strain your vocal cords and use a higher pitch compared to when pronouncing 'ㅈ'. ❗ Expect upper and lower teeth to touch for a moment as you begin pronouncing the ㅉ.

Stroke order	Font variations
	짜 짜 짜 짜 *Common digital font* *Common handwriting font*

Example

짜 쩌 쪼 쭈 쯔 찌 쨈 쬔

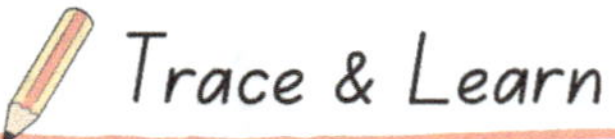 Trace & Learn

🔊 **Track 45**

ㅉ	ㅉ				
짜	짜				
쩌	쩌				
쪼	쪼				
쭈	쭈				

1

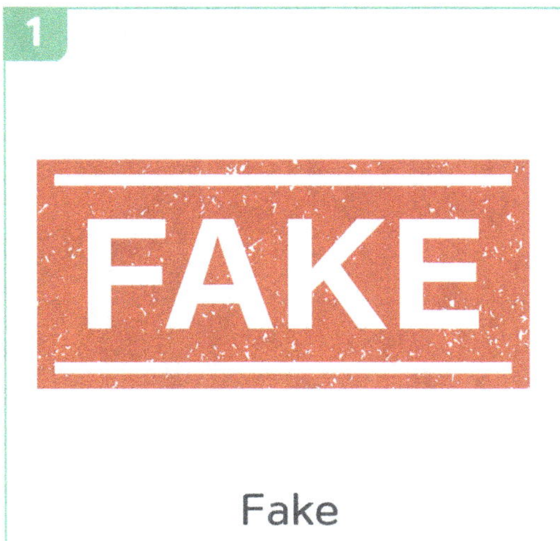

Fake

가 짜 가 짜

2

Jjigae (Korean stew)

찌 개 찌 개

3

Jjukkumi
(Webfoot octopus)

쭈 꾸 미
쭈 꾸 미

	Pronun-ciation	Writing Practice					
ㄲ	/k'/	ㄲ	ㄲ				
ㄸ	/t'/	ㄸ	ㄸ				
ㅆ	/p'/	ㅆ	ㅆ				
ㅃ	/s'/	ㅃ	ㅃ				
ㅉ	/tʃ'/	ㅉ	ㅉ				

		ㅏ	ㅓ	ㅗ	ㅡ	ㅣ	ㅐ	ㅔ
ㄲ		까						
ㄸ		떠						
ㅆ				쏘				
ㅃ				쁘				
ㅉ						찌		

읽기 연습
Reading Practice

🔊 **Track 46**

1. 다음 글자를 잘 듣고 소리 내어 읽어보세요.
Listen carefully and read out loud the following letters.

1	가	까	카	거	꺼
2	타	다	토	따	도
3	바	빠	파	뽀	포
4	사	싸	쏘	쇼	슈
5	차	자	짜	츄	쮸

2. 다음 음절을 잘 듣고 소리 내어 읽어보세요.
Listen carefully and read out loud the following syllables.

1	가요	까요	5	부리	뿌리
2	커요	꺼요	6	아빠가 아파요	아빠가 바빠요
3	타요	따요	7	자요 차요 짜요	
4	사요	싸요	8	다 타요 다 타	

1. 다음 글자를 잘 듣고 소리 내어 읽어보세요.

Listen carefully and read out loud the following letters.

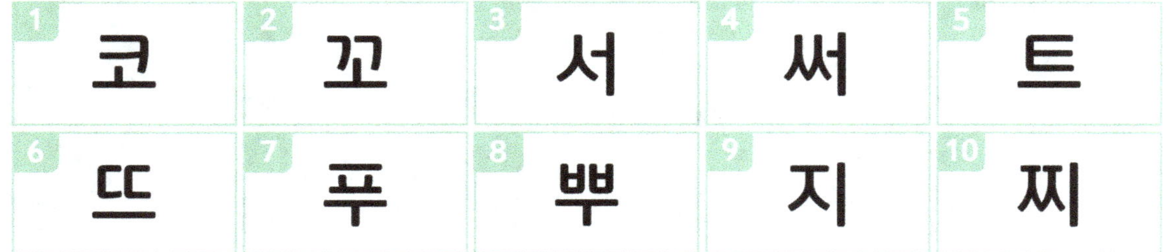

2. 다음을 잘 듣고 맞으면 O표, 틀리면 X표를 하세요.

Listen carefully and mark O for correct or X for incorrect.

3. 잘 듣고 맞는 글자에 O표 하세요.

Listen carefully and mark O on the correct letter.

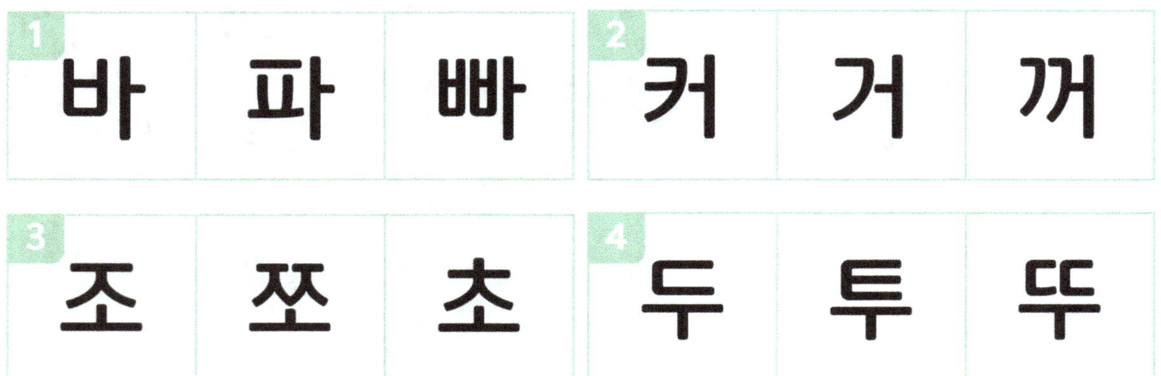

4. 잘 듣고 단어를 받아쓰세요.

Listen carefully and dictate the word.

1	
2	
3	
4	

5. 다음 그림에 알맞은 단어를 쓰세요.

Write the matched word under the picture.

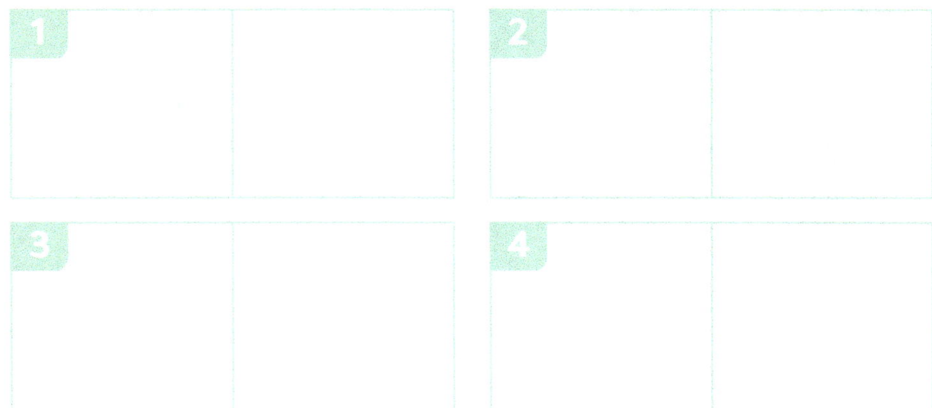

1	2	3
Rabbit	Kiss (lightly)	Jjigae (Korean stew)
4	5	6
Trash	Hair band	Cricket

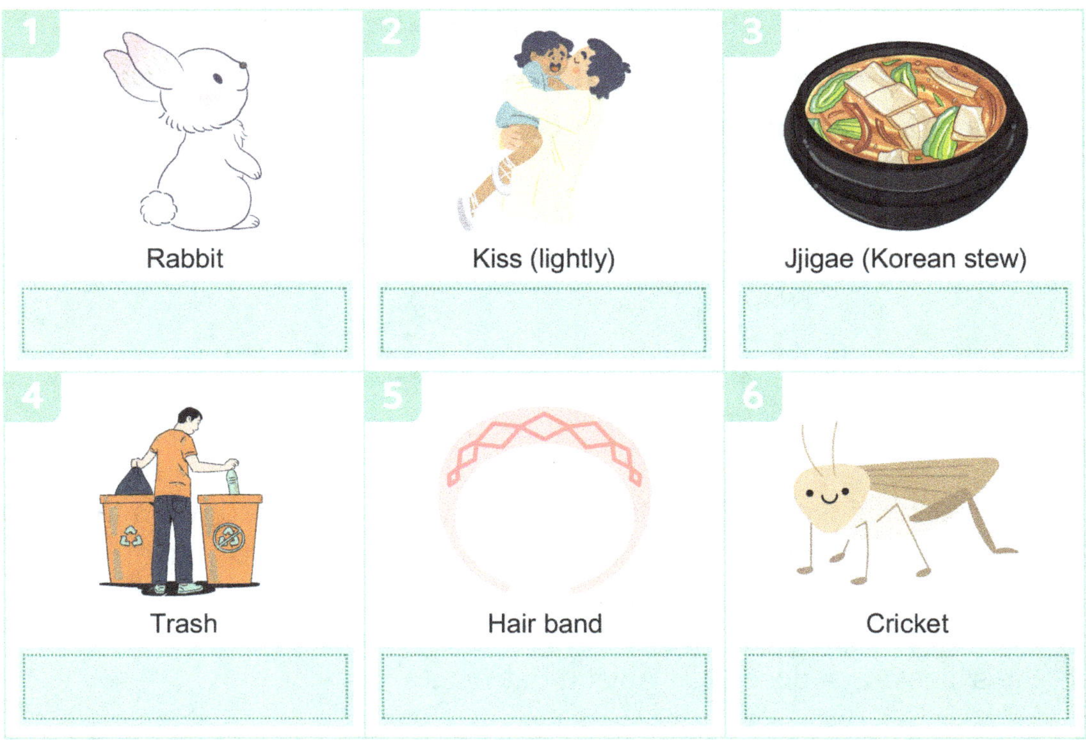

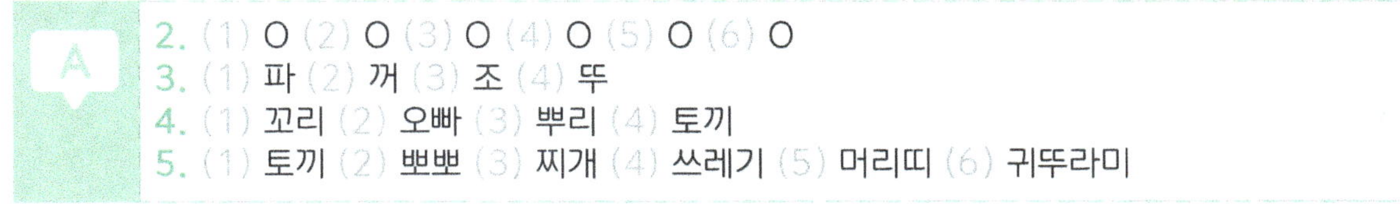

5. Batchim
(Consonant base / Final consonant)

받침

A Korean syllable's final consonant, also known as 'Consonant base,' is called 'Batchim'. When writing word in English, the letters are written in a row to form a word. However, keeping a square shape for each syllable is necessary in the Korean language. (Refer to page 13) Thus, **to keep a square shape, the batchim should be placed under the combination of a consonant and a vowel.**

Also, using the original term '받침 Batchim' is highly recommended when talking about it with Koreans. Most Koreans do NOT know the grammar terms made from English perspective.

Q Mark the syllable that does NOT have a batchim.

방	탄	소	년	단

The answer is '소'.

Types of Batchim

There are three types of Batchim depending on the combination.

Type	Single Batchim (홑받침)	Double Batchim (쌍받침)	Compound Batchim (겹받침)
Component	One single letter	Two same letters	Two different letters
Example	ㄱ, ㄴ, ㄷ, ㄹ, ㅁ, ㅂ, ㅅ, ㅇ, ㅈ, ㅊ, ㅋ, ㅌ, ㅍ, ㅎ	ㄲ, ㅆ	ㄳ, ㄵ, ㄶ, ㄺ, ㄻ, ㄼ, ㄽ, ㄿ, ㄾ, ㅀ, ㅄ

How to read Single & Double Batchim

(Refer to pages 142-143 to review how to read syllables with compound Batchim)

Do you know about the unique characteristics of the Korean language? While it has many single and double batchims, there are only seven distinct sounds. This is because some batchims are difficult to pronounce when followed by certain syllables. To simplify things, batchim sounds are grouped together based on how they are articulated by the vocal organ, and one easier pronunciation is used for the entire group.

- **Base pronunciation of Single & Double Batchim**

  When a word ends with a batchim or when the following letter doesn't affect the syllable's pronunciation, you can read batchim according to this rule.

Batchim	Pronunciation	IPA	Example
ㅇ	[ㅇ]	/ŋ/	[앙]: 앙
ㅁ	[ㅁ]	/m/	[암]: 암
ㄹ	[ㄹ]	/l/	[알]: 알
ㄴ	[ㄴ]	/n/	[안]: 안
ㄱ, ㅋ, ㄲ	[ㄱ]	/g/, /k/	[악]: 악, 악, 앆
ㄷ, ㅌ, ㅅ, ㅆ, ㅈ, ㅊ, ㅎ	[ㄷ]	/d/, /t/	[앋]: 앋, 앝, 앗, 았, 앚, 앛, 앟
ㅂ, ㅍ	[ㅂ]	/b/, /p/	[압]: 압, 앞

This book will guide you to the easiest order to learn and remember Batchim pronunciation. The order we will see in this book may be different from the one in other books. Please be aware of this as you study.

- **When a vowel follows a batchim: Linking occurs**

When batchim is followed by a vowel, the batchim shifts into the position of '○'.

(i.e.)

한 국 어
[한구거]
Korean language

월 요 일
[워료일]
Monday

있 어 요
[이써요]
~ exist(s)

강 아 지
/ŋ/
[강아지]
Puppy, Small dog

When the batchim '○' is followed by a vowel, it has a /ŋ/ sound. In this case, linking does NOT occur. (Refer to page 124)

(i.e.) 고양이[고양이] Cat, 영어[영어] English language

쌓 이 다
✗
[싸이다]
To pile up, be stacked

When the batchim 'ㅎ' is followed by a vowel, the batchim 'ㅎ' becomes silent. (Refer to page 137)

(i.e.) 좋아하다[조아하다] To like, 낳아요[나아요] ~give(s) birth

- **When a consonant follows a batchim: Other phenomena occur**

Many different phenomena may occur depending on the combination of letters. However, compared to other phenomena, aspiration and tensing phenomena occur more commonly. These two exhibit patterns similar to the principles to the consonant-creating principle (Flat-Aspirated-Tense consonant), which we have previously learned (Pages 104-105) (To learn in-depth, refer to pages 168-171)

1. Aspiration

When the batchim is ㄱ, ㄷ, ㅂ, or ㅈ and is followed by 'ㅎ' or vice-versa, those two consonants are merged and are pronounced in the next syllable.

(i.e.)

맏₊형
[마텽]
The eldest brother

2. Tensing

When the batchim is ㄱ, ㄷ, ㅂ, ㅅ or ㅈ and is followed by 'ㄱ, ㄷ, ㅂ, ㅅ or ㅈ', the consonant in the next syllable is pronounced as tense sound.

(i.e.)

학₊생
[학쌩]
Student

받침을 넣어 글자를 완성시켜 보세요.
Practice assembling letters with batchim

나		ㄴ		난			
라		ㄹ		랄			
마		ㅁ		맘			
아		ㅇ		앙			
가		ㄱ		각			
카		ㅋ		칵			
까		ㄲ		깎			
다	+	ㄷ	=	닫			
타		ㅌ		탈			
사		ㅅ		삿			
싸		ㅆ		쌌			
자		ㅈ		잦			
차		ㅊ		찾			
하		ㅎ		항			
바		ㅂ		밥			
파		ㅍ		팦			

Batchim	Tip for pronunciation
ㅇ	'ng' as in 'si**ng**[sɪŋ]' or 'so**ng**[sɑːŋ]'. ⚠ The linking does NOT occur with this batchim even if it is followed by a vowel.

Pronunciation	Font variations
IPA /ŋ/ Romanization [ng]	앙 앙 앙 앙

✏ **Let's read and write**

🔊 **Track 48**

1

병 아 리

병 아 리

Chick
[병아리]

2

냉 장 고

냉 장 고

Refrigerator
[냉장고]

Batchim	Tip for pronunciation
□	"m" as in "mo**m**[mɑːm]"

Pronunciation	Font variations
IPA /m/ Romanization [m]	맘 맘 맘 맘

✏️ Let's read and write

🔊 **Track 49**

1

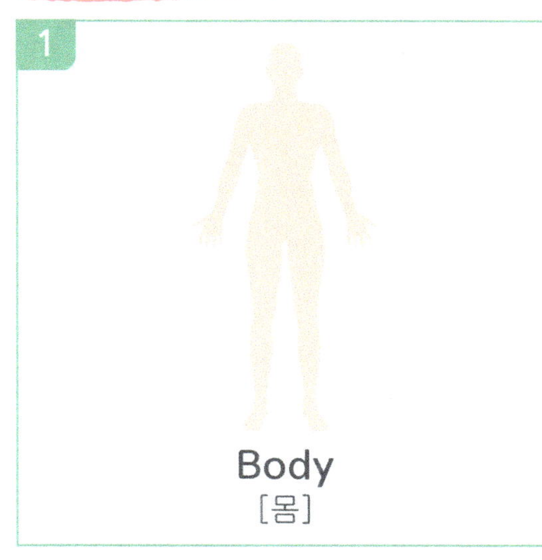

Body
[몸]

몸 몸

2

Heart, Mind
[마음]

마 음 마 음

125

Batchim	Tip for pronunciation
ㄹ	"l" as in "oi**l**[ɔɪl]" or "wi**ll**[wɪl]" ⚠ Bend your tongue a bit more to touch a little deeper area of your mouth when pronouncing batchim compared to when pronouncing it as the first consonant.

Pronunciation	Font variations
IPA /l/ Romanization [l]	랄 랄 *랄* 랄

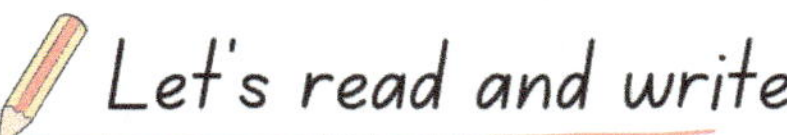

✏ *Let's read and write*

🔊 **Track 50**

1

Moon
[달]

달 달

2

Face
[얼굴]

얼 굴 얼 굴

Batchim	Tip for pronunciation
ㄴ	"n" as in "su**n**[sʌn]" or "me**n**[men]"

Pronunciation	Font variations
IPA /n/ Romanization [n]	난 난 난 난

✏️ Let's read and write

🔊 **Track 51**

1

Money
[돈]

돈	돈		

2

Soldier
[구닌]

군	인	군	인

Batchim	Tip for pronunciation
ㄱ	"g" as in "bi**g**/bɪg/" or "do**g**/dɑːg/", but without your jaw moving again at the end; "k" as in "coo**k**/kʊk/" or "wo**k**/wɑːk/", but without a puff of air sound.

Pronunciation	Font variations
IPA /g/, /k/ *Romanization* [g], [k]	각　각　각　각

✏️ Let's read and write

1

Soup
[국]

국	국		

2

Dining table
[식탁]

식	탁	식	탁

Batchim	Tip for pronunciation
ㅋ	See ㄱ (page 128)

Pronunciation	Font variations
IPA /g/, /k/ Romanization [g], [k]	칵 칵 칵 칵

✏️ Let's read and write

🔊 **Track 53**

1

녘 녘

In the direction of
[녘]

2

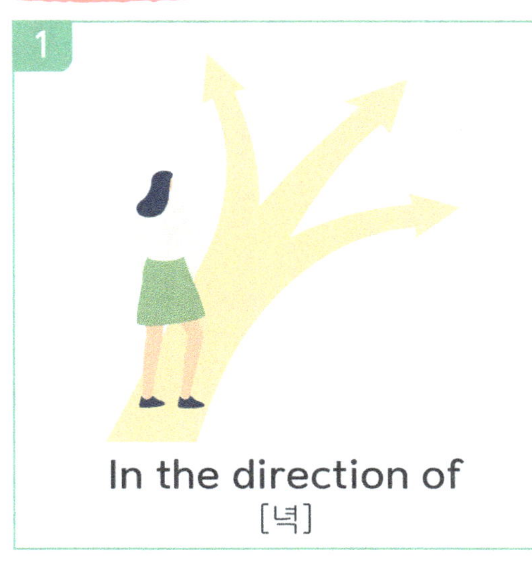

부 억 부 억

Kitchen
[부억]

Batchim	Tip for pronunciation
ㄲ	See ㄱ (page 128)

Pronunciation	Font variations
IPA /g/, /k/ Romanization [g], [k]	깎 깎 깎 깎

✏️ Let's read and write

🔊 **Track 54**

1

Outside
[박]

밖	밖		

2

Tteokbokki
(Sweet red chili seasoned rice cake)
[떡뽀끼]

떡	볶	이
떡	볶	이

Batchim	Tip for pronunciation
ㄷ	"d" as in "go**d** /gɑːd/" or "an**d** /ænd/", but without your tongue moving away at the end; "t" as in "bu**t** /bət/" or "cu**t** /kʌt/", but without a puff of air sound.

Pronunciation	Font variations
IPA /d/ /t/ Romanization [d] [t]	닫 닫 닫 닫

✏️ Let's read and write

🔊 **Track 55**

1

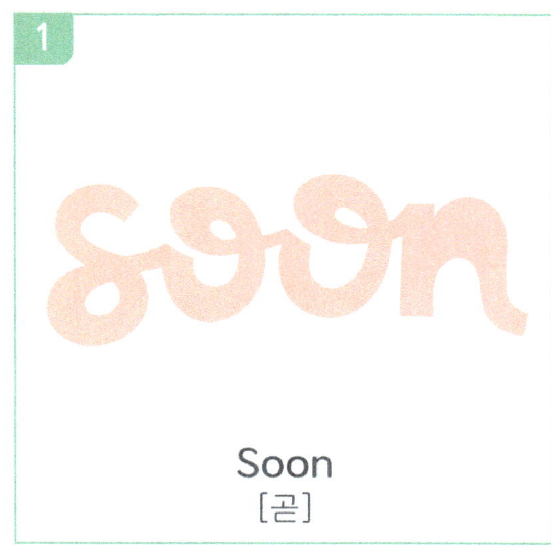

Soon
[곧]

곧 곧

2

Batchim
[받침]

받 침 받 침

Batchim	Tip for pronunciation
ㅌ	See "ㄷ" (Page 131)

Pronunciation	Font variations
IPA　　　　/d/ /t/ Romanization　[d] [t]	탙　탙　탙　탙

 Let's read and write

 Track 56

1

End
[끝]

끝	끝		

2

Field / Farm
[밭]

밭	밭		

Batchim	Tip for pronunciation
ㅅ	See "ㄷ" (Page 131)

Pronunciation	Font variations
IPA /d/ /t/ Romanization [d] [t]	삿 삿 삿 삿

Let's read and write

🔊 Track 57

1

Clothes
[옫]

옷 옷

2

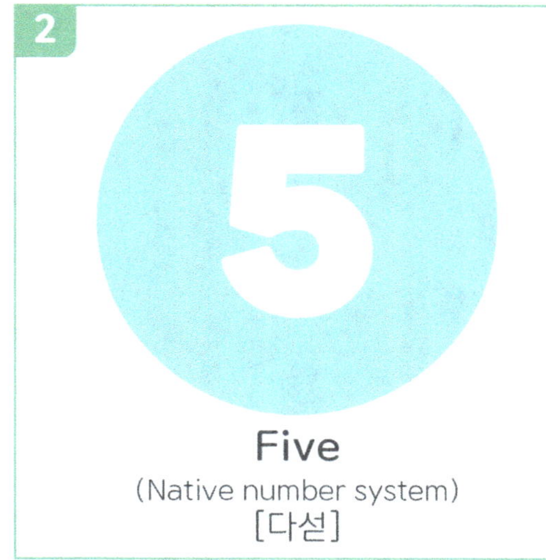

Five
(Native number system)
[다섣]

다 섯 다 섯

Batchim	Tip for pronunciation
ㅆ	See "ㄷ" (Page 131)

Pronunciation	Font variations
IPA /d/ /t/ Romanization [d] [t]	쌌 쌌 쌌 쌌

 Let's read and write

 **Track 58**

1

~ Went to
[가써요]

갔	어	요
갔	어	요

2

To exist
[읻따]

있	다	있	다

Batchim	Tip for pronunciation
ㅈ	See "ㄷ" (Page 131)

Pronunciation	Font variations
IPA /d/ /t/ Romanization [d] [t]	잦 잦 잦 잦 Common digital font · Common handwriting font

 Let's read and write

Track 59

1

Daytime
[낟]

낮 낮

2

Oversleep
[늗짬]

늦 잠 늦 잠

Batchim	Tip for pronunciation
ㅊ	See "ㄷ" (Page 131)

Pronunciation	Font variations
IPA /d/ /t/ Romanization [d] [t]	찾 찾 찾 찾 Common digital font · Common handwriting font

 **Let's read and write**

Track 60

1

Flower
[꼳]

꽃	꽃		

2

Light
[빋]

빛	빛		

Batchim	Tip for pronunciation
ㅎ	See "ㄷ" (Page 131) ⚠ When the batchim 'ㅎ' is followed by a vowel, the batchim 'ㅎ' becomes silent. (Refer to pages 122, 166). Otherwise, it is pronounced [ㄷ]

Pronunciation	Font variations
IPA /d/ /t/ Romanization [d] [t]	핳 핳 핳 핳

✏ Let's read and write

🔊 **Track 61**

1

~ like/likes
[조아해요]

좋	아	해	요
좋	아	해	요

2

Hieut
[히읃]

히	읗	히	읗

Batchim	Tip for pronunciation
ㅂ	"b" as in "jo**b** /dʒɑːb/" or "we**b**/web/", but without opening your lips at the end; "p" as in "cu**p**/kʌp/" or "li**p**/lɪp/", but without giving a puff of air at the end.

Pronunciation	Font variations
IPA /b/ /p/ Romanization [b] [p]	밥　밥　밥　밥

 Let's read and write

1

Cooked rice / Meal
[밥]

밥	밥		

2

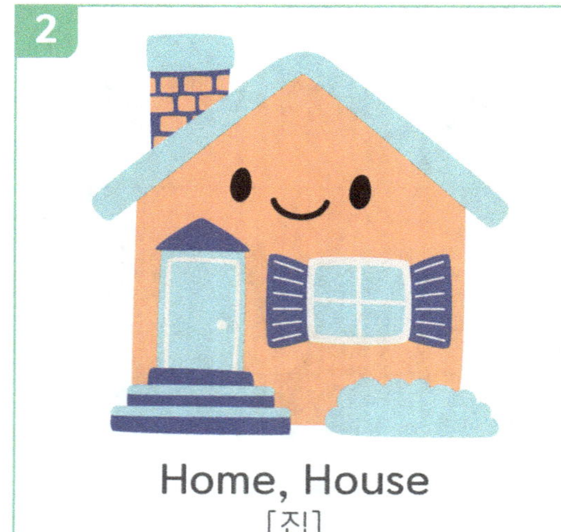

Home, House
[집]

집	집		

Batchim	Tip for pronunciation
ㅍ	See "ㅂ" (Page 138)

Pronunciation	Font variations
IPA /b/ /p/ Romanization [b] [p]	팥 팥 팥 팥

✏️ Let's read and write

🔊 Track 63

1

Leaf
[입]

잎	잎		

2

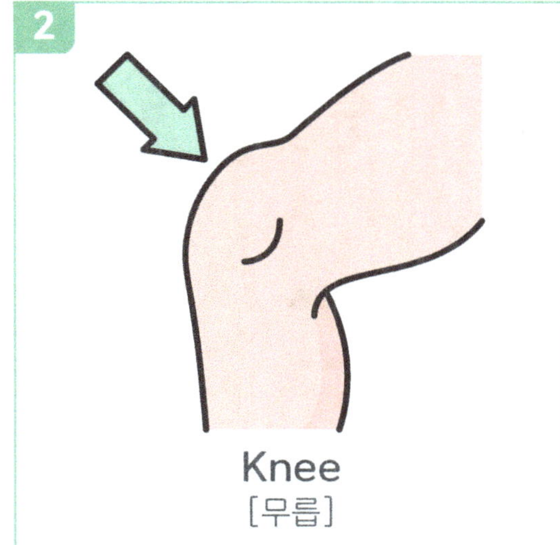

Knee
[무릅]

무	릎	무	릎

1. 다음 글자를 잘 듣고 소리 내어 읽어보세요.
Listen carefully and read out loud the following letters.

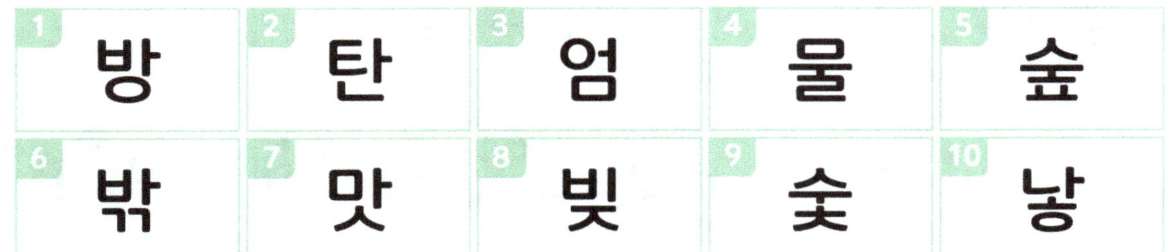

2. 다음을 잘 듣고 맞으면 O표, 틀리면 X표를 하세요.
Listen carefully and mark O for correct or X for incorrect.

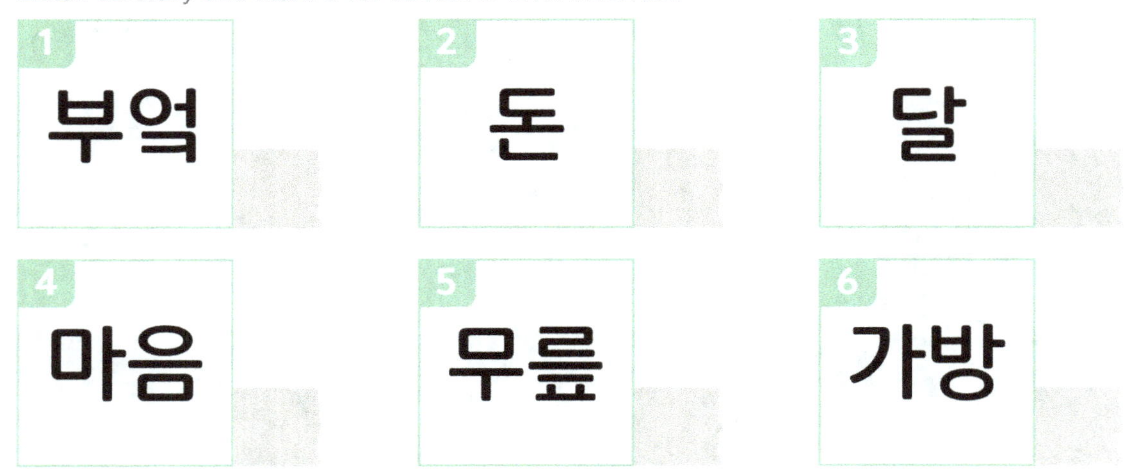

3. 잘 듣고 맞는 글자에 O표 하세요.
Listen carefully and mark O on the correct letter.

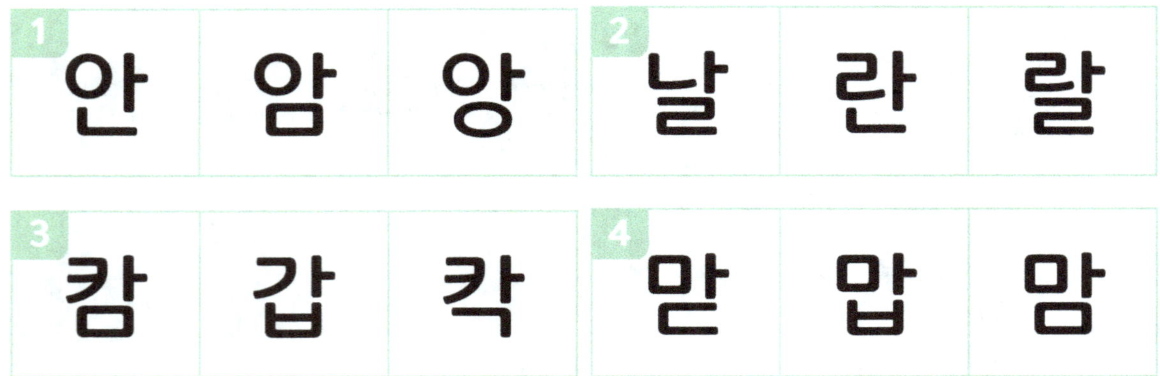

4. 잘 듣고 단어를 받아쓰세요.

Listen carefully and dictate the word.

1	
2	
3	
4	

5. 다음 그림에 알맞은 단어를 쓰세요.

Write the matched word under the picture.

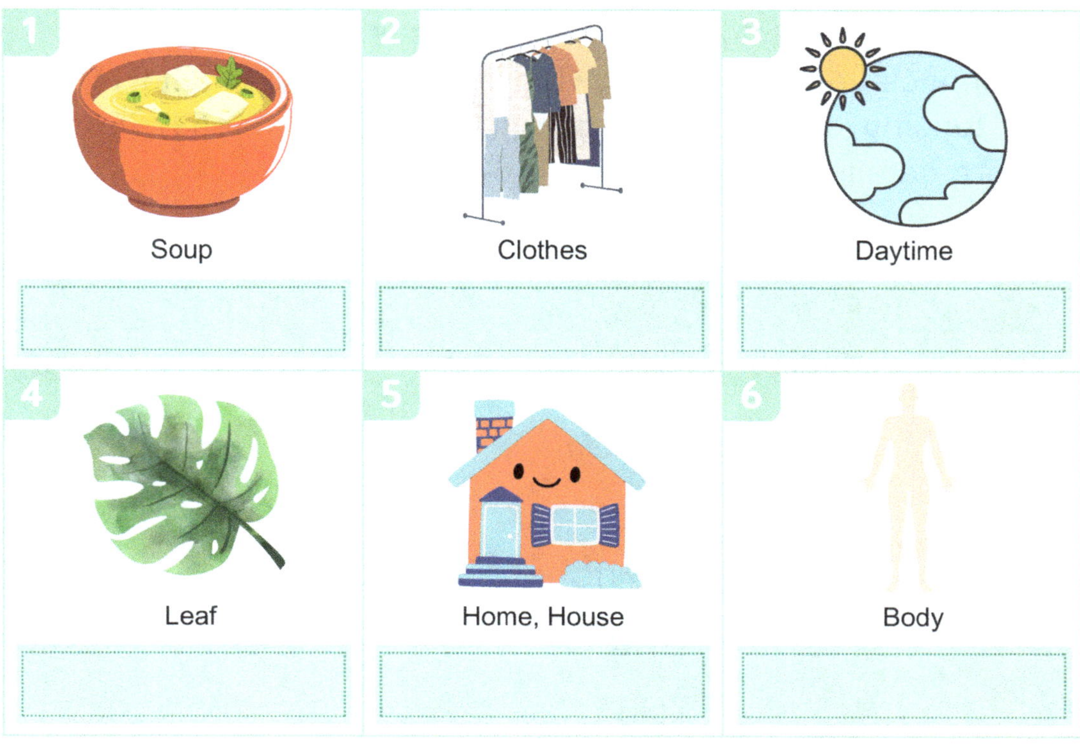

1. Soup
2. Clothes
3. Daytime
4. Leaf
5. Home, House
6. Body

A

2. (1) X [부업] (2) O (3) O (4) X [마을] (5) O (6) X [가발]
3. (1) 안 (2) 란 (3) 칵 (4) 맙
4. (1) 얼굴 (2) 군인 (3) 식탁 (4) 받침
5. (1) 국 (2) 옷 (3) 낮 (4) 잎 (5) 집 (6) 몸

6. Compound Batchim

겹받침

Compound batchim (겹받침) refers to **a combination of two different batchims**. When positioned in the final syllable, compound batchim is pronounced using its representative sound, which is typically the first of the two batchims. However, it plays a crucial role when another syllable follows. In most cases, it influences the pronunciation of the following syllable, creating linking or tensing sounds or triggering other phenomena. (For more details, refer to pages 166-171).

When former batchim is pronounced			When latter batchim is pronounced		
Compound Batchim	Pronunciation	Example	Compound Batchim	Pronunciation	Example
ㄱㅅ	ㄱ	몫[목], 넋[넉]	ㄹㄱ	ㄱ	닭[닥], 흙[흑]
ㄴㅈ	ㄴ	앉다[안따]	ㄹㅁ	ㅁ	젊다[점따]
ㄴㅎ	ㄴ	많다[만타]	ㄹㅂ*	ㅂ	밟다[밥따]
ㄹㅂ*	ㄹ	여덟[여덜]	ㄹㅍ	ㅍ[ㅂ]	읊다[읍따]
ㄹㅅ	ㄹ	곬[골]			
ㄹㅌ	ㄹ	핥다[할따]			
ㄹㅎ	ㄹ	싫다[실타]			
ㅂㅅ	ㅂ	없다[업따]			

* The Batchim '래' can be pronounced in two ways; ㄹ/r, l/ or ㅂ /b, p/, depending on the syllable. In most cases, the syllables ending with the batchim 래 are pronounced ㄹ/r, l/. However, the syllables '밟' and '넓' are pronounced ㅂ/b, p/.

(i.e.)

짧 다
[짤따]
To be short

밟 다
[밥따]
To step on

How to pronounce it accurately?

- **When a vowel comes after compound batchim: Linking occurs**

The second letter of the compound batchim is shifted to the initial position of the following syllable when it is followed by the consonant 'ㅇ(이응)', which is a silent sound.

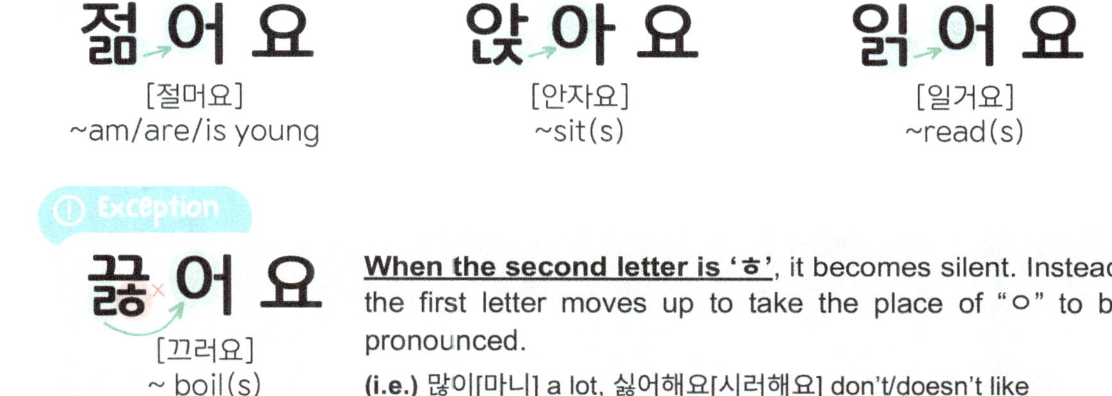

젊 어 요
[절머요]
~am/are/is young

앉 아 요
[안자요]
~sit(s)

읽 어 요
[일거요]
~read(s)

ⓘ Exception

끓 어 요
[끄러요]
~ boil(s)

When the second letter is 'ㅎ', it becomes silent. Instead, the first letter moves up to take the place of "ㅇ" to be pronounced.

(i.e.) 많이[마니] a lot, 싫어해요[시러해요] don't/doesn't like

- **When a consonant follows batchim: Other phenomena occur**

Various phenomena may occur depending on the combination of letters. Aspiration and tensing comparably largely occur, in particular. To know more about these, refer to pages 168-171.

1. Aspiration	2. Tensing
When the last letter of the compound batchim is ㄱ, ㄷ, ㅂ, or ㅈ and it's followed by 'ㅎ' or vice-versa, those two letters are merged and are pronounced in the next syllable as aspirated sound.	When the last letter of the compound batchim is ㄱ, ㄷ, ㅂ, or ㅈ and it's followed by 'ㄱ, ㄷ, ㅂ or ㅈ', those two letters are pronounced as tense sound in the next syllable.

(i.e.)

넓+히 다
[널피다]
To widen, broaden

(i.e.)

앉+다
[안따]
To sit

Batchim	Tip for pronunciation
ㄳ	• **As the final syllable:** ㄱ is pronounced as its representative sound. • **When followed by a vowel:** ㄱ is pronounced within the syllable. ㅅ is shifted to the following syllable. • **When followed by a consonant:** ㅅ may affect the next syllable's pronunciation in various ways. (How? Check out pages 168-181)

Representative sound	Font variations
ㄱ /g/ /k/ (Refer to page 128)	몫　몫　몫　몫

✏️ *Let's read and write*

🔊 **Track 65**

1

(noun) Share
[목]

몫	몫		

2

Soul
[넉]

넋	넋		

Batchim	Tip for pronunciation
ㄴㅈ	• **As the final syllable:** ㄴ is pronounced as its representative sound. • **When followed by a vowel:** ㄴ is pronounced in the syllable. ㅈ is shifted to the following syllable. • **When followed by a consonant:** ㅈ may affect the next syllable's pronunciation in various ways. (How? Check out pages 168-181)

Representative sound	Font variations
ㄴ /n/ (Refer to page 127)	앉　앉　앉　앉 Common digital font　　Common handwriting font

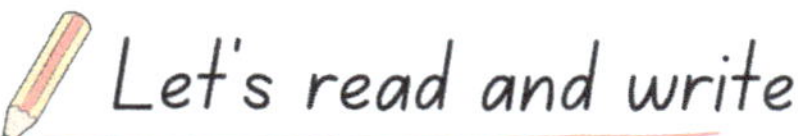

✏️ Let's read and write

🔊 **Track 66**

1

앉 아 요

~ sit(s) down
[안자요]

2

얹 다 얹 다

To put (something) on
[언따]

Batchim	Tip for pronunciation
ㄴㅎ	• **As the final syllable:** ㄴ is pronounced as its representative sound. • **When followed by a vowel:** ㄴ is shifted to the following syllable because <u>batchim ㅎ becomes silent.</u> • **When followed by a consonant:** ㅎ may affect the next syllable's pronunciation in various ways. (How? Check out pages 168-181)

Representative sound	Font variations			
ㄴ /n/ (Refer to page 127)	많	많	많	많

Let's read and write

◀ **Track 67**

1

괜	찮	아	요
괜	찮	아	요

~ am/are/is okay
[괜차나요]

2

많	다	많	다

To have a lot/many/much
[만타]

Batchim	Tip for pronunciation
ㄺ	• **As the final syllable:** ㄱ is pronounced as its representative sound. • **When followed by a vowel:** ㄹ is pronounced in the syllable. ㄱ is shifted to the following syllable. • **When followed by a consonant:** ㄱ may affect the next syllable's pronunciation in various ways. (How? Check out pages 168-181)

Representative sound	Font variations
ㄱ /g/ (Refer to page 128)	읽 읽 읽 읽

✏️ Let's read and write

🔊 **Track 68**

1

Chicken
[닥]

닭	닭		

2

~ read(s)
[일거요]

읽	어	요
읽	어	요

Batchim	Tip for pronunciation
20	• **As the final syllable:** ㅁ is pronounced as its representative sound. • **When followed by a vowel:** ㄹ is pronounced in the syllable. ㅁ is shifted to the following syllable. • **When followed by a consonant:** ㅁ may affect the next syllable's pronunciation in various ways. (How? Check out pages 168-181)

Representative sound	Font variations			
ㅁ /m/ (Refer to page 125)	앎	앎	앎	앎

✏️ Let's read and write

🔊 **Track 69**

1

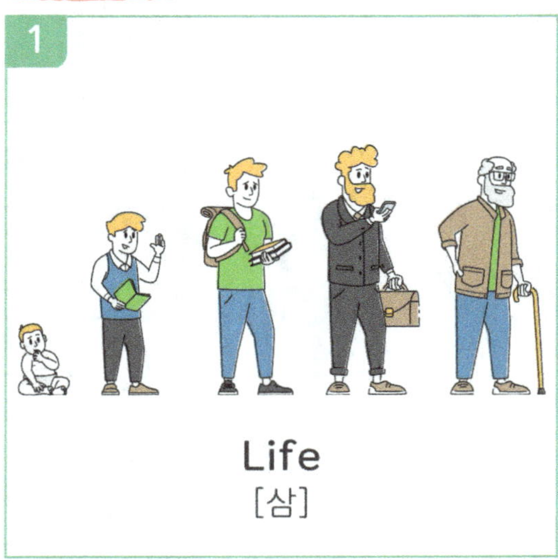

Life
[삼]

삶	삶		

2

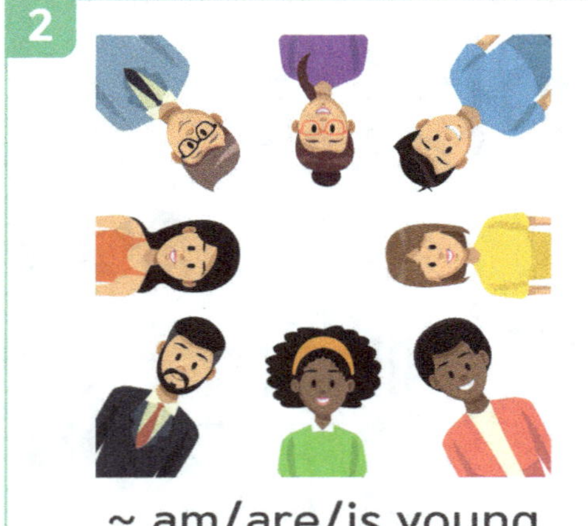

~ am/are/is young
[절머요]

젊	어	요
젊	어	요

Batchim	Tip for pronunciation
ㄼ	• **As the final syllable:** ㄹ or ㅂ is pronounced as its representative sound in the syllable depending on the word. (Refer to page 143) • **When followed by a vowel:** ㄹ is pronounced in the syllable. ㅂ is shifted to the following syllable. • **When followed by a consonant:** ㅂ may affect the next syllable's pronunciation in various ways. (How? Check out pages 168-181)

Representative sound	Font variations
ㄹ /r/ /l/ or ㅂ /b/ /p/ (Refer to page 126, 138)	덟　덟　덟　덟

✏️ Let's read and write

🔊 **Track 70**

1

8

Eight(8)
(Native number system)
[여덜]

여	덟	여	덟

2

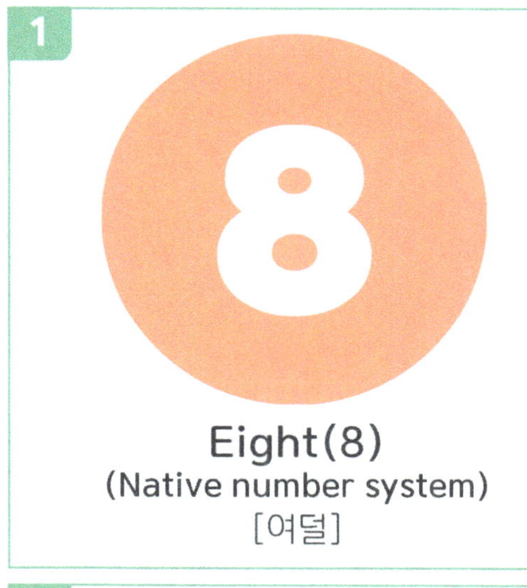

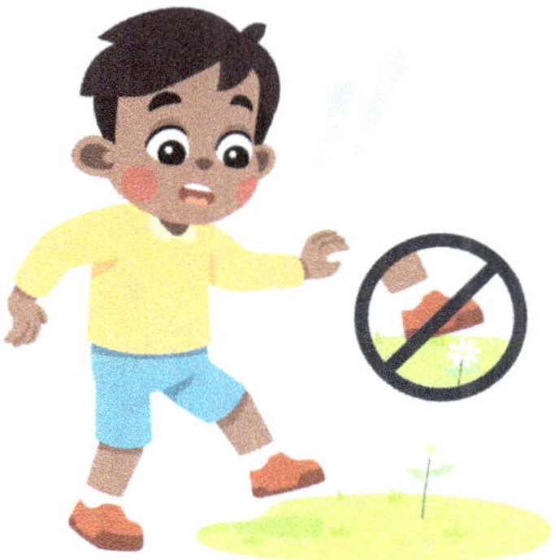

To step on
[밥따]

밟	다	밟	다

Batchim	Tip for pronunciation
라	• **As the final syllable:** ㄹ is pronounced as its representative sound. • **When followed by a vowel:** ㄹ is pronounced in the syllable. ㅅ is shifted to the following syllable. • **When followed by a consonant:** ㅅ may affect the next syllable's pronunciation in various ways. (How? Check out pages 168-181)

Representative sound	Font variations
ㄹ /r/ /l/ (Refer to page 126)	곬　곬　곬　곬

✏️ Let's read and write

🔊 **Track 71**

1

A set or fixed way/direction
[골]

곬　곬

* There are not many words ending with this batchim in Korean.

Batchim	Tip for pronunciation
ㄹㅌ	• **As the final syllable:** ㄹ is pronounced as its representative sound. • **When followed by a vowel:** ㄹ is pronounced in the syllable. ㅌ is shifted to the following syllable. • **When followed by a consonant:** ㅌ may affect the next syllable's pronunciation in various ways. (How? Check out pages 168-181)

Representative sound	Font variations
ㄹ /r/ /l/ (Refer to page 126)	핥 핥 핥 핥

✏️ Let's read and write

🔊 **Track 72**

1

To lick
[할따]

핥	다	핥	다

2

~ Skim(s) through
[훌터요]

훑	어	요
훑	어	요

Batchim	Tip for pronunciation
ㄿ	• **As the final syllable:** ㄹ is pronounced as its representative sound. • **When followed by a vowel:** ㄹ is pronounced in the syllable. ㅍ is shifted to the initial position of the following syllable. • **When followed by a consonant:** ㅍ may affect the next syllable's pronunciation in various ways. (How? Check out pages 168-181)

Representative sound	Font variations
ㄹ /r/ /l/ (Refer to page 126)	읊 읊 읊 읊

✏️ *Let's read and write*

 🔊 **Track 73**

1

~ recite(s)
[을퍼요]

읊	어	요
읊	어	요

* There are not many words ending with this batchim in Korean.

Batchim	Tip for pronunciation
ㄹㅎ	• **As the final syllable:** ㄹ is pronounced as its representative sound. • **When followed by a vowel:** ㄹ is shifted to the following syllable <u>because Batchim ㅎ becomes silent.</u> • **When followed by a consonant:** ㅎ may affect the next syllable's pronunciation in various ways. (How? Check out pages 168-181)

Representative sound	Font variations
ㄹ /r/ /l/ (Refer to page 126)	옳 옳 옳 옳

 Let's read and write

🔊 **Track 74**

1

~do/does not like
[시러요]

싫	어	요
싫	어	요

2

To boil
[끌타]

끓	다	끓	다

Batchim	Tip for pronunciation
ㅄ	• **As the final syllable:** ㅂ is pronounced as its representative sound. • **When followed by a vowel:** ㅂ is pronounced in the syllable. ㅆ is pronounced as the initial consonant of the next one. (Refer to page 166) • **When followed by a consonant:** ㅅ may affect the next syllable's pronunciation in various ways. (How? Check out pages 168-181)

Representative sound	Font variations			
ㅂ /b/ /p/ (Refer to page 138)	값	값	값	값

✏️ Let's read and write

🔊 **Track 75**

1

Value
[갑]

값	값		

2

없	어	요
없	어	요

~ not exist(s)
[업써요]

받침을 넣어 글자를 완성시켜 보세요.

Practice assembling letters with batchim.

모		ㄱㅅ	몫	
아		ㄴㅈ	앉	
마		ㄴㅎ	많	
이		ㄹㄱ	읽	
저		ㄹㅁ	젊	
더	+	ㄹㅂ =	덟	
고		ㄹㅅ	곬	
하		ㄹㅌ	핥	
으		ㄹㅍ	읊	
시		ㄹㅎ	싫	
어		ㅂㅅ	없	

1. 다음 글자를 잘 듣고 소리 내어 읽어보세요.

Listen carefully and read out loud the following letters.

1	2	3	4	5
몫	앉	많	닭	젊

6	7	8	9	10
덥	핥	싫	없	읖

2. 다음을 잘 듣고 맞으면 O표, 틀리면 X표를 하세요.

Listen carefully and mark O for correct or X for incorrect.

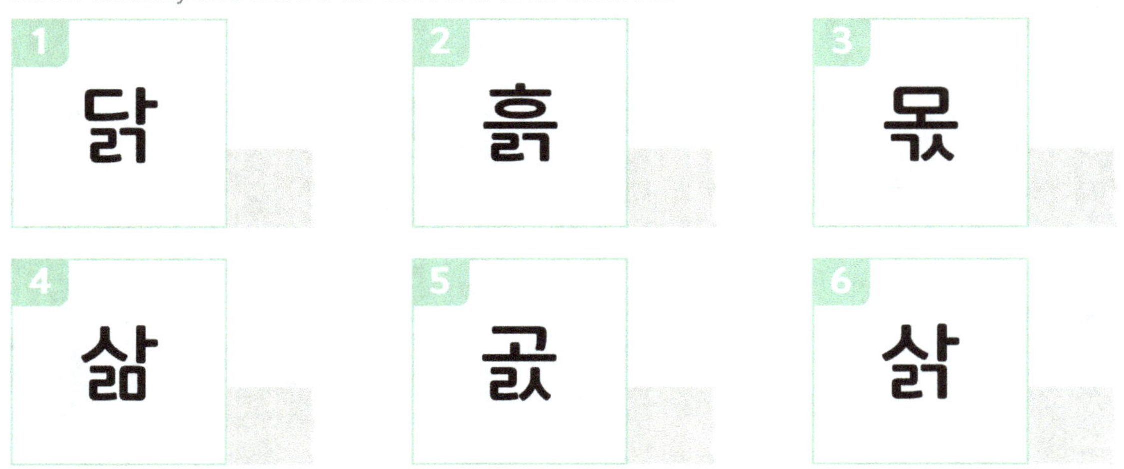

3. 잘 듣고 맞는 글자에 O표 하세요.

Listen carefully and mark O on the correct letter.

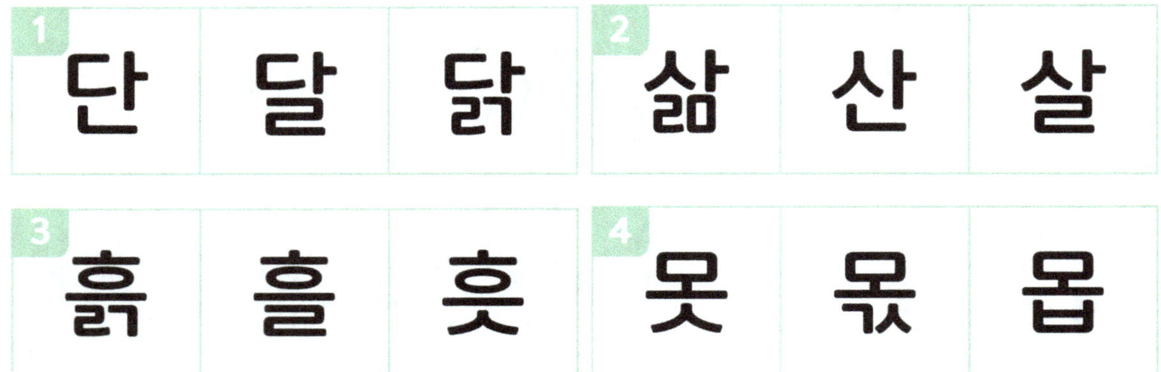

4. 잘 듣고 단어를 받아쓰세요.

5. 다음 그림에 알맞은 단어를 쓰세요.

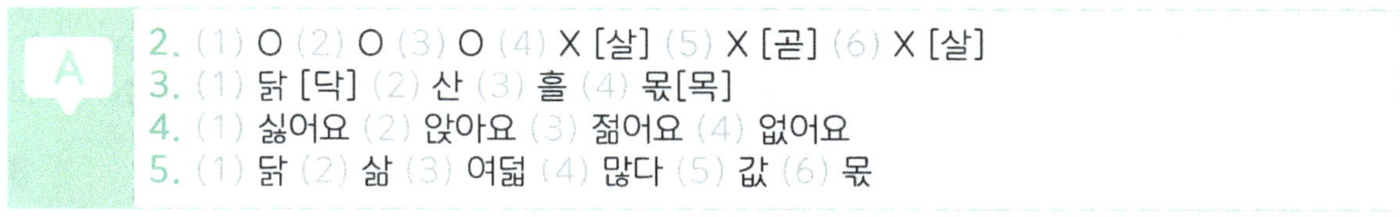

Bright and Dark Vowel
한국어의 양성 모음과 음성 모음

Categorizing bright and dark vowels is a theoretical concept but also has practical implications in everyday Korean conversations. Typically, bright vowels are paired with other bright vowels, while dark vowels are paired with other dark vowels. This pairing affects the overall tone of the conversation. When a word consists of bright vowels, it conveys a sense of brightness and positivity, and the opposite is also true. There are many examples of this phenomenon in the Korean language, which can be easily observed in daily expressions.

Vowel " ㅏ "

The sun is positioned on the east of a person, representing the common knowledge that the sun rises from the east, indicating the start of the day and filling the earth with brightness, matching the brightness of the vowel " ㅏ ".

Vowel "ㅗ"

The sun is positioned above the landscape, representing the noon when the sun's brightness illuminates the land. It echoed in the brightness of the vowel "ㅗ".

Vowel " ㅓ "

The sun is positioned on the west of a person, representing the common knowledge that the sunsets to the west indicate the end of the day filling the earth with darkness, matching the darkness of the vowel " ㅓ ".

Vowel "ㅜ"

The sun is positioned below the horizon, representing the night when darkness spreads across the land. It echoes in the darkness of the vowel "ㅜ".

1 Words describing a sound

The Korean language has different ways to describe a laughing sound, such as 하하(호호) or 허허(후후, 흐흐, 히히). However, these two words have different connotations for native Koreans. 하하 is associated with a burst of pleasant, happy laughter due to the bright vowel, whereas 허허 is linked to sarcastic, bitter, or wicked laughter due to the dark vowel. The pitch of the laughing sound can also affect the perception of the sound. If the pitch is normal or high, it is more likely to be heard as 하하 by Koreans. Conversely, if the pitch is lower than usual, it is usually described as 허허.

하하(호호)

pleasant and happy laughter

허허(후후, 흐흐, 히히)

sarcastic, bitter, or wicked laughing

② Colors and shapes

It carries similar connotations when describing colors in Korean; using bright or dark vowels depends on the feeling associated with the color. Bright and warm colors are typically described with bright vowels, while darker and cooler colors or an unpleasant combination of colors are described with dark vowels.

Also, we can describe the shapes differently using vowels. If you use bright vowels, the word can carry a positive and bright tone, while dark vowels give people a somewhat negative and dark tone.

알록달록한

colorful

얼룩덜룩한

mottled, spotted, stained

통통한

chubby

뚱뚱한

fatty

However, these days, this pattern is slowly going away due to the fast pace of new words being created. As a result, newer words do not always follow this phenomenon.

koreanstudycafe.official

koreanstudycafe.official
오늘 처음으로 삼겹살 쌈을 먹어 봤어요. 정말 맛있었어요!
Today, I tried sam–gup–sal–ssam(pork belly wrap)
for the first time. It was so good.

SEOUL
ADMITTED
JUL 16
AIRPORT

Korean Pronunciation
한국어의 발음

Korean Pronunciation

The following section will explain the organized patterns and categorization of Korean pronunciation processed differently compared to its spelling. If you consider it as pronunciation rules, you might feel overwhelmed and frustrated because many cases don't follow the established rules, making it difficult to learn the Korean language. Thus, it's important to note that **this isn't a rigid rule but rather a pattern of pronunciation changes developed by Koreans who value efficiency and adaptability.**

Why some words are pronounced differently?

The pronunciation of all phonetic languages has evolved and optimized over time to pronounce effectively and deliver the exact meaning without confusion. Therefore, it is common to see such patterns in any phonetic language, such as English, French, Spanish, etc. Linking sound exists to be pronounced easily and keep the flow of smooth conversation. Therefore, we pronounce "Stop it" sounds like [STA piT] instead of how it is written. Why do many languages allow such a phenomenon? That is because it is more efficient. Thus, the Korean language also allows many pronunciation phenomena for the same reason.

Tips on how to study Korean pronunciation

Acknowledge it's impossible to convey Korean sounds accurately using English sounds

No language can perfectly describe the other language's pronunciation because every language has only as many letters or sounds as needed. Thus, remember the native speaker's pronunciation and ignore the English romanization. English romanization will eventually hinder your pronunciation improvement.

Check out the pronunciation of the word that you see for the first time

Even though you can pronounce most words right after learning Hangul with this book, some are pronounced in a way you never expected. Thus, if you are unsure of the pronunciation, utilize online tools such as an online Korean dictionary where you can listen to the pronunciation of each word.

Do NOT try to memorize all the pronunciation rules

At first, you may set goals to memorize all the pronunciation rules in this book. However, thinking of all the rules when reading Korean sentences will be exhausting. To begin with, take a quick look at all the chapters without feeling obligated to memorize them. Next, focus on practicing your reading skills. If you encounter unfamiliar words with unexpected pronunciations, refer to the related patterns in this book and review them as many times as necessary, even if you have already studied them a few times.

Read it aloud

Repeatedly reading aloud allows your brain, vocal cords, and related muscles to become more proficient and adjust to new sounds. Not only does the reading out-aloud method improve your pronunciation, but it also aids in memorizing Korean words. Consider this process similar to polishing up new skills. While you learn a skill theoretically, you need to train your body to master it until it becomes an automatic reaction.

Be positive! Be confident!

Be confident with your current pronunciation and focus on improving your pronunciation gradually through practice. If you practice enough, your pronunciation will gradually improve, sounding like a native speaker.

It is not easy even for native Korean speakers to pronounce the vowel '의' correctly in all situations. Therefore, the pronunciation of this vowel varies depending on where it is. Most Koreans pronounce the vowel in alternative ways in daily conversation because it involves a lot of tongue movement to pronounce the original pronunciation of '의'. However, the original pronunciation is also acceptable and understandable by Koreans.

How to pronounce properly

1 When it's in the first syllable, pronounce the vowel as [ㅢ].

2 When it's paired with a consonant(except for 'ㅇ'), pronounce the vowel as [ㅣ].

3 When it's not the first syllable, you can also pronounce the vowel as [ㅣ].

4 When it is a possessive particle*, you can also pronounce the vowel as [ㅔ].

* Particles in Korean
The Korean language has particles indicating the grammatical function of the previous word.
(i.e., subject marking particles 이 and 가, object marking particles 을 and 를)

Examples (Each example corresponds to the number provided above).

1	**2**	**3**	**4-1**	**4-2**
의자	희망	주의	나의	강의
[의자]	[히망]	[주이/주의]	[나에/나의]	[강에/강의]
Chair	Hope	Caution	My (– of me)	–of river

다음 단어들을 듣고 따라 읽으세요.
Listen to the words and repeat them after the narrator.

1 의사 [의사] Doctor	**2** 의견 [의견] Opinion
3 무늬 [무니] (mark, design) Pattern	**4** 희다 [히다] To be white
5 회의 [회ː이] Meeting, conference	**6** 예의 [예이] Manners, etiquette, politeness
7 우리의 [우리에] Our (- of us)	**8** 누구의 [누구에] Whose (-of whom)
9 한국의 문화 [한구게 무놔] The culture of Korea / Korean culture	**10** 민주주의의 의미 [민주주이에 의미] The meaning of democracy

* Remember, you can also pronounce using the original pronunciation of "의".
  i.e.) 민주주의의 의미 [민주주의의 의미 / 민주주이에 의미]

This pattern is the most widely used in terms of Korean pronunciation. Since the consonant '○' is silent, it is easy to be replaced with the sound of the batchim from the right before the syllable for a smooth flow of the conversation. However, the spelling can never change, even though the pronunciation is changed.

How to pronounce properly

1 When **a single or double Batchim** is followed by '○,' shift up the batchim to the place of '○', and pronounce it as its original sound.

2 When **a compound Batchim** meets the '○' of the next syllable, move up the second letter of the compound Batchim to the place of '○' and pronounce accordingly.

Examples *(Each example corresponds to the number provided above).*

1

단어	있어	강아지*	쌓이다**
[다너]	[이써]	[강아지]	[싸이다]
Word, Vocabulary	~ exist/exists	Puppy, small dog	To pile up

* When two '○' encounter, pronounce the word as it is supposed to.
** When **the Batchim is '○'** and the next consonant is '○', the batchim becomes silent.

2

앉아요	젊어요	없어요*	끓어요**
[안자요]	[절머요]	[업써요]	[끄러요]
~ sit/sits	~ am/are/is young	~ not exist/exists	~ boil/boils

* **If the second letter is 'ㅅ'**, pronounce [ㅆ] in the next syllable.
** **If the second letter is 'ㅎ'** (i.e., 'ㄹㅎ' or 'ㄴㅎ'), ignore 'ㅎ' and shift up the first letter to the place of '○.'

Why 'ㅎ' becomes silent?

The sound of ㅎ is WEAKER than other consonants. You can also see the same phenomenon in English, where the consonant 'H' becomes easily silent or sounds weaker (i.e. hour[aʊr], school[sku:l], ghost[goʊst]). For this reason, 'ㅎ' becomes silent to avoid difficult pronunciation.

Exceptional cases

There are a few exceptional cases that do not show this phenomenon to deliver the original meaning of the word. (i.e., 맛없어요[맏업서요], 헛웃음[허두슴])

다음 단어들을 듣고 따라 읽으세요.

Listen to the words and repeat them after the narrator.

1 **음악** [으막] Music	**2** **할아버지** [하라버지] Grandfather
3 **오징어** [오징어] Squid	**4** **좋아요** [조아요] ~ am/are/is good
5 **잊어버렸어요** [이저버려써요] ~ forgot	**6** **닮았어요** [달마써요] ~resemble(s), take(s) after (someone)
7 **잃어버렸어요** [이러버려써요] ~ lost	**8** **넓어요** [널버요] ~ is wide, large, spacious

Aspiration means adding wind pressure to words. Do you remember the principle of the Korean aspirated consonants? (If not, refer to page 35) The same phenomenon can be seen where 'the batchim ㄱ, ㄷ, ㅂ, or ㅈ' meets 'ㅎ' or vice-versa.

How to pronounce properly

1 Batchim ㄱ(ㄺ), ㄷ, ㅂ(ㄼ), ㅈ(ㄵ) + 'ㅎ'　Batchim [-] + [ㅋ, ㅌ, ㅍ, ㅊ]

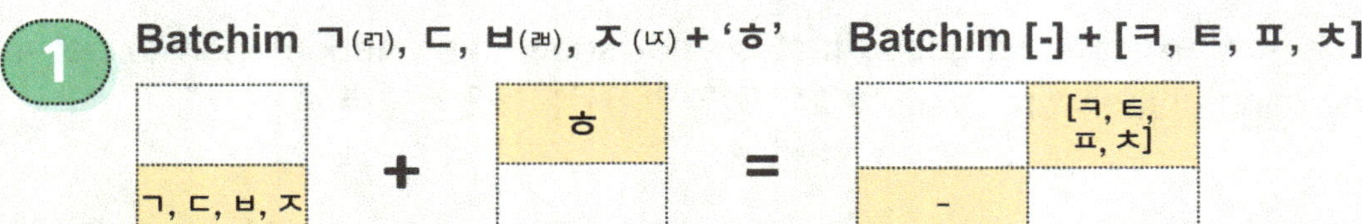

2 Batchim 'ㅎ(ㄶ, ㅀ)' + ㄱ, ㄷ, ㅂ, ㅈ　Batchim [-] + [ㅋ, ㅌ, ㅍ, ㅊ]

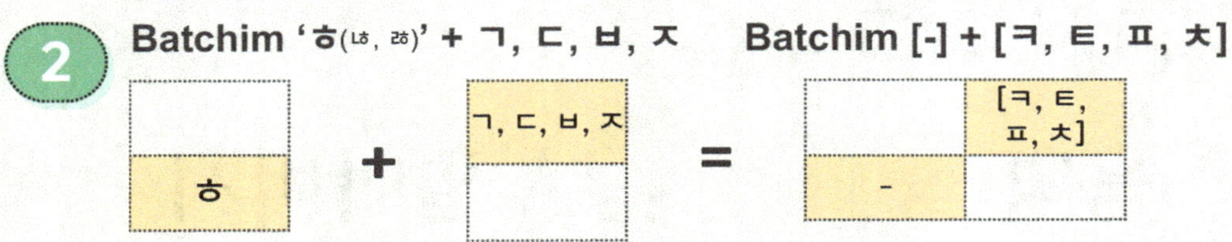

Examples *(Each example corresponds to the number provided above).*

1

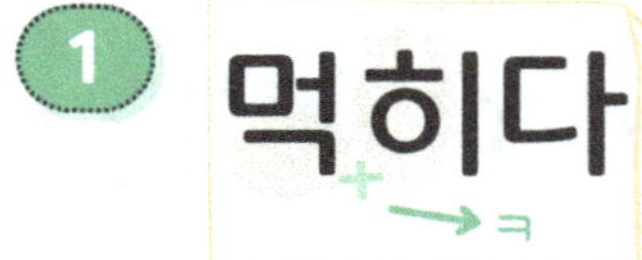

[머키다]

To be eaten

[마텽]

The eldest brother

[널피다]

To widen, broaden

앉히다

[안치다]

To make (someone) sit

2

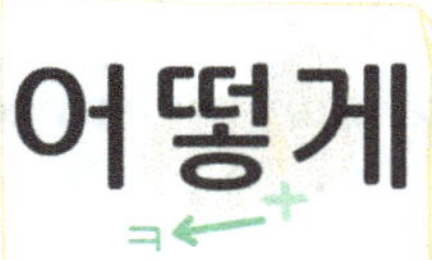

[어떠케]

How

좋다

[조타]

To be good, to like

괜찮지?

[괜찬치]

~ am/are/is okay, right?

[실타]

To dislike, hate

다음 단어들을 듣고 따라 읽으세요.
Listen to the words and repeat them after the narrator.

1 **까맣다** [까마타] To be black	**2** **이렇게** [이러케] Like this, this way
3 **많지 않아요** [만치 아나요] ~not exist / exists	**4** **싫다고 했어요** [실타고 해써요] ~ said that ~ hate/hates
5 **축하** [추카] Celebration, congratulation	**6** **입학** [이팍] Entrance into a school
7 **꽂히다** [꼬치다] To be stuck (with sharp object)	**8** **좁히다** [조피다] To narrow, close (on)

Do you remember flat consonants 'ㄱ, ㄷ, ㅂ, ㅅ and ㅈ'? When a flat consonant batchim 'ㄱ(ㄲ, ㅋ, ㄳ, ㄺ), ㄷ(ㅅ, ㅆ, ㅈ, ㅊ, ㅌ), ㅂ(ㅍ, ㄼ, ㄿ, ㅄ)' followed by another flat consonant, the followed flat consonant becomes a tense sound. (Refer to page 104)

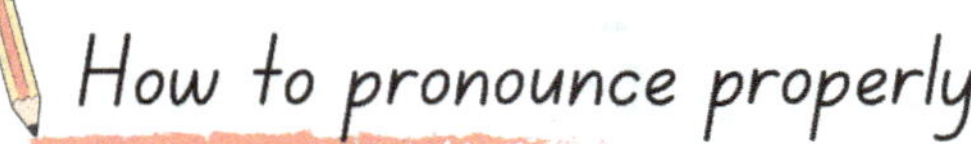
How to pronounce properly

✓ **Batchim ㄱ,ㄷ,ㅂ + ㄱ,ㄷ,ㅂ,ㅅ,ㅈ = [ㄲ,ㄸ,ㅃ,ㅆ,ㅉ]**

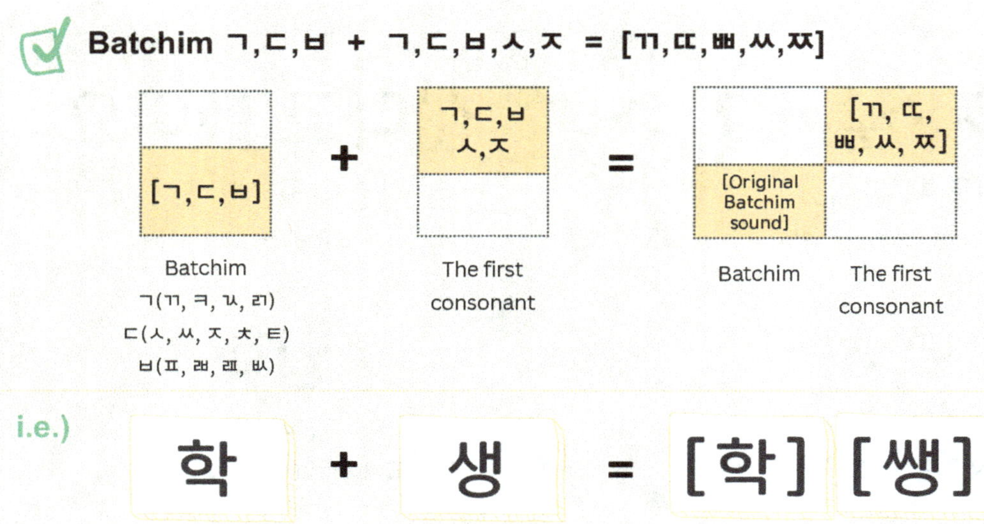

i.e.) 학 + 생 = [학] [쌩]

Some other tensing patterns are shown depending on the grammatical features of this phenomenon. All these patterns are **OPTIONAL** phonological phenomena. It depends on the word or expression.

Case (a) When Hanja words* ending with 'ㄹ' + 'ㄷ, ㅅ, ㅈ' = [ㄸ, ㅆ, ㅉ]

i.e., 갈등[갈뜽] conflict, 발전[발쩐] development

*한자(Hanja) refers to Chinese characters used in the Korean writing system. Hanja was historically used in Korean writing alongside the native Korean script.

Case (b) When verb stems ending with 'ㄴ, ㄹ, ㅁ' + 'ㄱ, ㄷ, ㅅ, ㅈ' = [ㄲ, ㄸ, ㅆ, ㅉ]

i.e., 신고[신꼬] wear and, 앉다[안따] to sit

Case (c) When a verb ending is '을/ㄹ' + 'ㄱ, ㄷ, ㅂ, ㅅ, ㅈ' = [ㄲ, ㄸ, ㅃ, ㅆ, ㅉ]

i.e., 먹을 거야[머글꺼야] ~ will eat, 할 수 있어[할쑤이써] ~ can do

다음 단어들을 듣고 따라 읽으세요.
Listen to the words and repeat them after the narrator.

1

학생
[학쌩]
Student

2

약국
[약꾹]
Pharmacy

3

첫사랑
[천싸랑]
First love

4

꽃집
[꼳찝]
Flower shop

5

식당
[식땅]
Restaurant

6

책방
[책빵]
Bookstore, bookshop

7

듣다
[듣따]
To listen

8

젊고
[점꼬]
~ am/are/is young and
Refer to case (b) on previous pages

9

물가
[물까]
Market price
Refer to case (a) on previous page

10

읽을 거야
[일글 꺼야]
~ will read (casual tone)
Refer to case (c) on previous page

When ㄷ/ㅌ meets 이/히, the latter ones are pronounced as [지/치] instead of [디/티] due to palatalization. To understand this phenomenon, see the illustration of vocal organs on the right side. The spot where the syllable '이/히' is pronounced is closer to the spot where the consonant 'ㅈ/ㅊ' is pronounced than the one for 'ㄷ/ㅌ'. Thus, our tongue can move less to pronounce such cases. Also, this is a common sound-changing phenomenon in many other languages including English. Take an example of the phrases "and you?" and "last year". You may pronounce them like /ənjyu/ and /læschir/ than /ənd-yu/ and /læst-ir/, right? This also happens for the same reason.

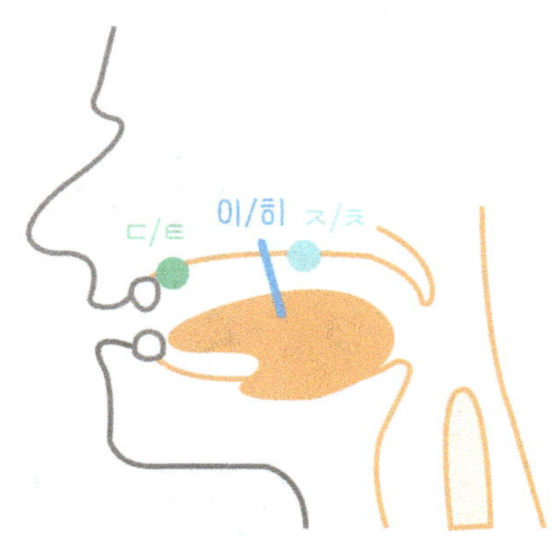

The spots where your tongue is touched when pronouncing them

How to pronounce properly

(1) **Batchim 'ㄷ' + 이 = Batchim [ㅡ] + [지]**

| ㄷ | **+** | 이 | **=** | ㅡ | [지] |

(2) **Batchim 'ㄷ' + 히 = Batchim [ㅡ] + [치]**

| ㄷ | **+** | 히 | **=** | ㅡ | [치] |

(3) **Batchim 'ㅌ (ㄾ)' + 이 = Batchim [ㅡ] + 치**

| ㅌ | **+** | 이 | **=** | ㅡ | [치] |

* *There are no circumstances where batchim ㅌ combines with 히 in Korean*

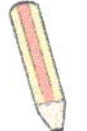
Examples *(Each example corresponds to the number provided on the previous page).*

1

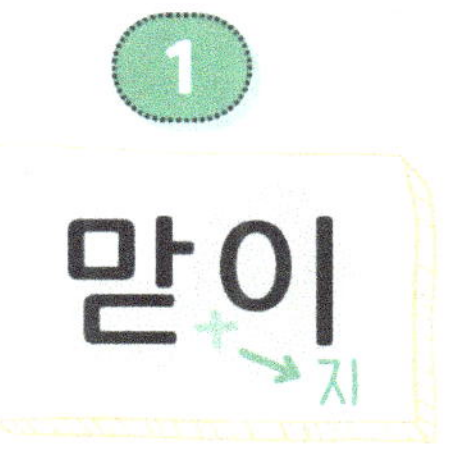

[마지]

Firstborn, the eldest (child)

2

[다치다]

To be shut, to be closed

3

[끄치]

End, tip, edge
+ subject marking particle

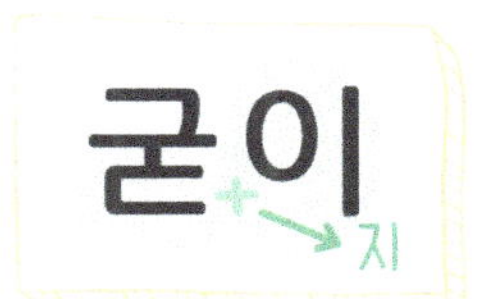

[구지]

~ bother(s) to do something

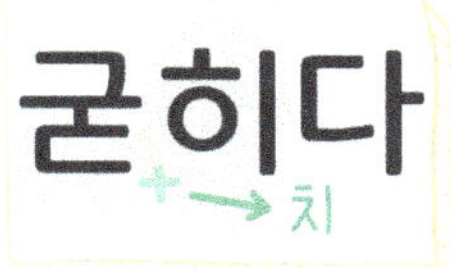

[구치다]

To make (something) hard,
to solidify

[가치]

Together, along with

다음 단어들을 듣고 따라 읽으세요.

Listen to the words and repeat them after the narrator.

1 해돋이 [해도지] Sunrise	**2** 미닫이 [미다지] Sliding door
3 걷히다 [거치다] To clear up (tax etc.) to be collected/gathered	**4** 묻히다 [무치다] To be buried, to be surrounded by
5 밑이 [미치] The bottom + subject marking particle	**6** 밭이 [바치] Farm + subject marking particle

Nasalization means that non-nasal-sounding consonants are pronounced as nasal sounds, which occur when air flows through the nose while you make a sound in the mouth. In Korean, there are plosive consonants(ㄱ, ㄷ, ㅂ), which are pronounced by the airflow being disturbed in our mouth. When those consonants meet with nasal-sounding consonants(비음), which are ㄴ, ㅁ, ㅇ, they are pronounced like nasal sounds for ease of pronunciation. When attempting to pronounce a nasal consonant followed by a plosive consonant, it is impossible to do so smoothly without halting the airflow of each syllable. This inefficiency requires extra tongue movement and can disrupt conversation. Therefore, Koreans opt to replace the plosive consonants with nasal sounds to maintain efficiency in conversation.

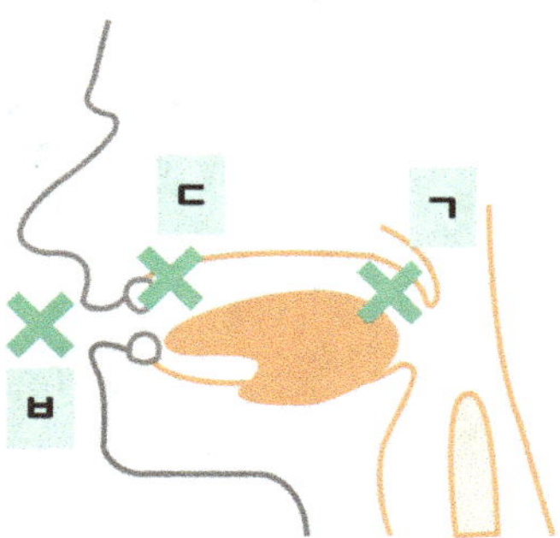

The air-flow of plosive sound consonants

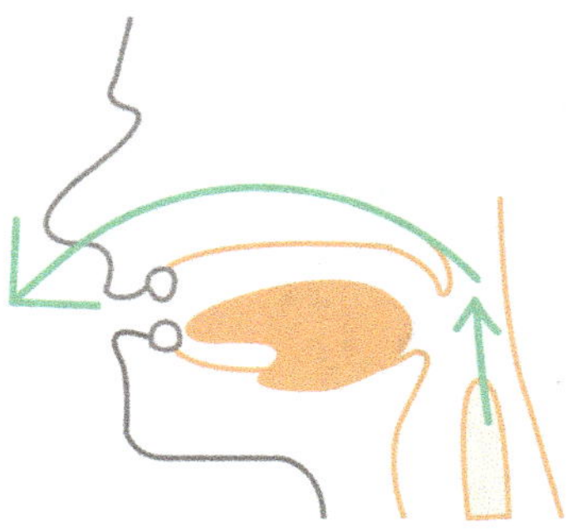

The air-flow of nasal sound consonants

ㄱ The tongue root does not touch the palate but moves upward, obstructing vocal cord sounds.

ㄷ The sound is produced when the tip of the tongue touches the roof of the mouth behind the upper teeth, interfering with the sound from the vocal cords.

ㅂ The sound coming from the vocal cords is interrupted by the lower and upper lips colliding with each other.

ㄴ ㅁ ㅇ The sound coming from the vocal cords travels through the rear nostrils, creating a sound.

How to pronounce properly

(1) **Batchim 'ㄱ'** (ㄲ, ㅋ, ㄳ, ㄺ) **+ ㄴ, ㅁ = Batchim [ㅇ] + ㄴ, ㅁ**

(2) **Batchim 'ㄷ'** (ㅅ, ㅆ, ㅈ, ㅊ, ㅌ, ㅎ) **+ ㄴ, ㅁ = Batchim [ㄴ] + ㄴ, ㅁ**

(3) **Batchim 'ㅂ** (ㅍ, ㄼ, ㄿ, ㅄ)**' + ㄴ, ㅁ = Batchim [ㅁ] + ㄴ, ㅁ**

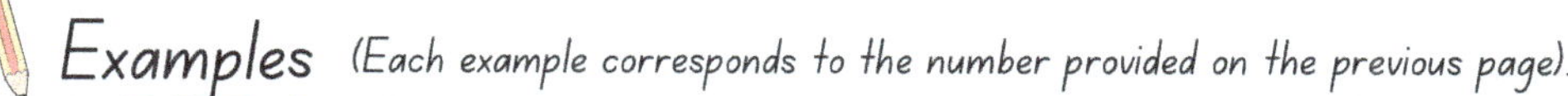

✏️ *Examples* *(Each example corresponds to the number provided on the previous page).*

다음 단어들을 듣고 따라 읽으세요.
Listen to the words and repeat them after the narrator.

The consonants 'ㄴ' and 'ㄹ' have strong connections. To correctly pronounce them, the tip of our tongue should touch the hard palate. However, the movement of the tongue differs between the two sounds. When attempting to pronounce them, you may notice that the tongue's movement for 'ㄹ' is more complex than that of 'ㄴ'. As a result, when 'ㄹ' is paired with other consonants that require excessive movement to produce the sound, it is often replaced with ㄴ.

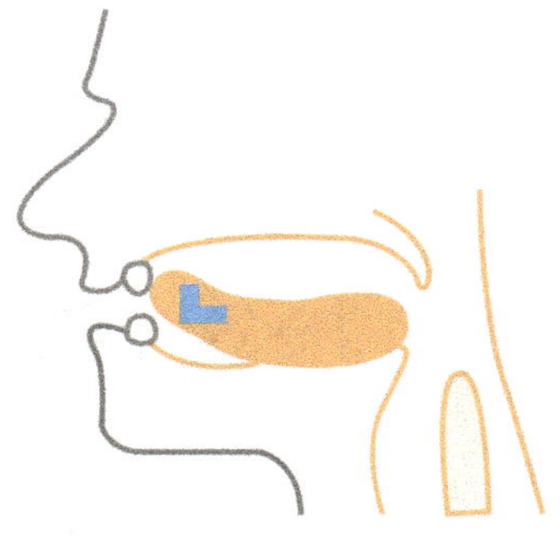

The tongue's movement to pronounce 'ㄴ'

The tongue lightly touches the roof of the mouth behind the teeth, then quickly pulls down to create a sound.

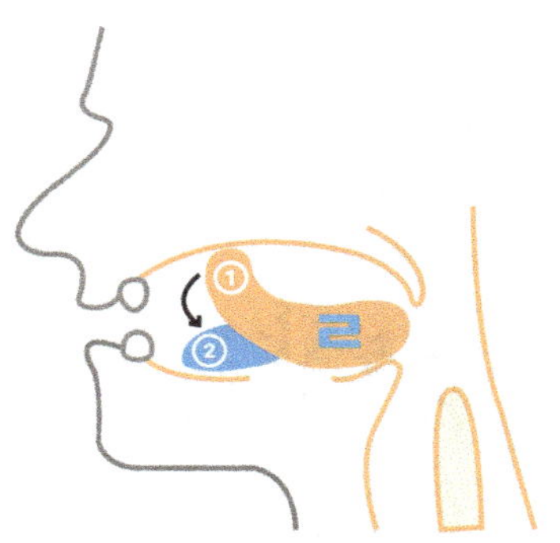

The tongue's movement to pronounce 'ㄹ'

Pronounce it by lightly touching the roof of your mouth (in the middle between your throat and your gum) with your tongue tip.

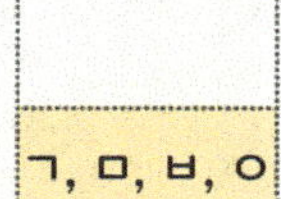 **How to pronounce properly**

Batchim 'ㄱ, ㅁ, ㅂ, ㅇ' + 'ㄹ' = Batchim [ㄱ, ㅁ, ㅂ, ㅇ] + [ㄴ]

	ㄹ		[ㄴ]
ㄱ, ㅁ, ㅂ, ㅇ	**+**	=	[ㄱ, ㅁ, ㅂ, ㅇ]

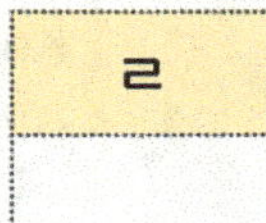 **Examples** *(Each example corresponds to the number provided above).*

침략	종로	석류	협력
[침냑]	[종노]	[석뉴 → 성뉴]*	[협녁 → 혐녁]*
Invasion	Jongno (the oldest major area in Seoul)	Pomegranate	Cooperation

* The pronunciation is changed once more according to the nasalization (Page 174). As you see here, it is possible to be applied more than one phenomenon in one word.

다음 단어들을 듣고 따라 읽으세요.

Listen to the words and repeat them after the narrator.

1 음료수
[음뇨수]
Drink, beverage

2 대통령
[대통녕]
President of a nation

3 정류장
[정뉴장]
Station, stop

4 수업료
[수업뇨 → 수엄뇨]*
Tuition

5 기억력
[기억녁 → 기엉녁]*
Memory

6 컵라면
[컵나면 → 컴나면]*
Instant cup ramen

* "Nasalization" also occurs in these examples. (Refer to page 174)

 # Lateralization (유음화 현상)

As mentioned in the previous chapter, there is a strong connection between the consonants 'ㄴ' and 'ㄹ'. But what happens when 'ㄴ' and 'ㄹ' meet each other? Well, an interesting process takes place. When 'ㄴ' and 'ㄹ' meet, 'ㄴ' is absorbed into 'ㄹ', resulting in the pronunciation of both consonants as [ㄹ+ㄹ], regardless of the order in which they appear.

How to pronounce properly

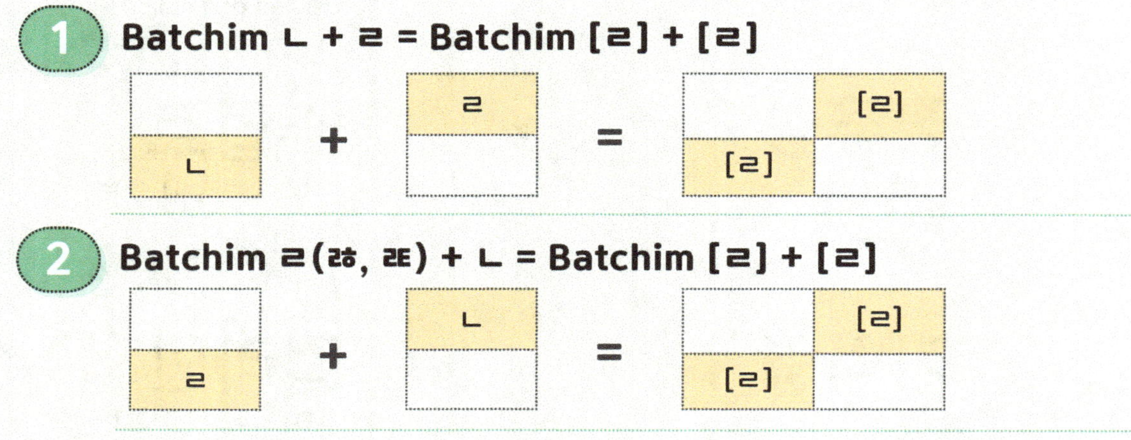

1 Batchim ㄴ + ㄹ = Batchim [ㄹ] + [ㄹ]

2 Batchim ㄹ(ㅀ, ㄾ) + ㄴ = Batchim [ㄹ] + [ㄹ]

Examples *(Each example corresponds to the number provided above).*

[날로]
Heater

[열락]
Contact, call, get in touch with

[실래]
Indoor, interior

[설랄]
Seollal
Lunar New Year's Day

⚠ **Exception**

Please note that there are a few exceptions that do not follow such a phenomenon. (i.e., 생산량[생산냥] production, 입원료[이뭔뇨] hospitalization cost). Although this way of pronunciation takes much more tongue movement, which is considered inefficient, very few words do not follow lateralization to deliver the meaning clearly.

다음 단어들을 듣고 따라 읽으세요.
Listen to the words and repeat them after the narrator.

1 신랑 [실랑] (bride's) groom	**2** 편리하다 [펼리하다] To be convenient, handy, easy
3 생일날 [생일랄] Birthday	**4** 물냉면 [물랭면] Mul-naengmyeon (Korean cold buckwheat noodles)
5 발을 핥는 개 [바를 할른 개] A dog that licks her paw	**6** 앓는 소리 [알른 소리] A groan, moan

When combining words to form compound or derivative words, if the pronunciation of a part changes significantly and makes it difficult for people to understand the original word or meaning, it may result in miscommunication. To avoid such problems, Koreans use the consonant 'ㄴ' as a bridge to connect the two parts. See below for an example of how this works.

How to pronounce properly

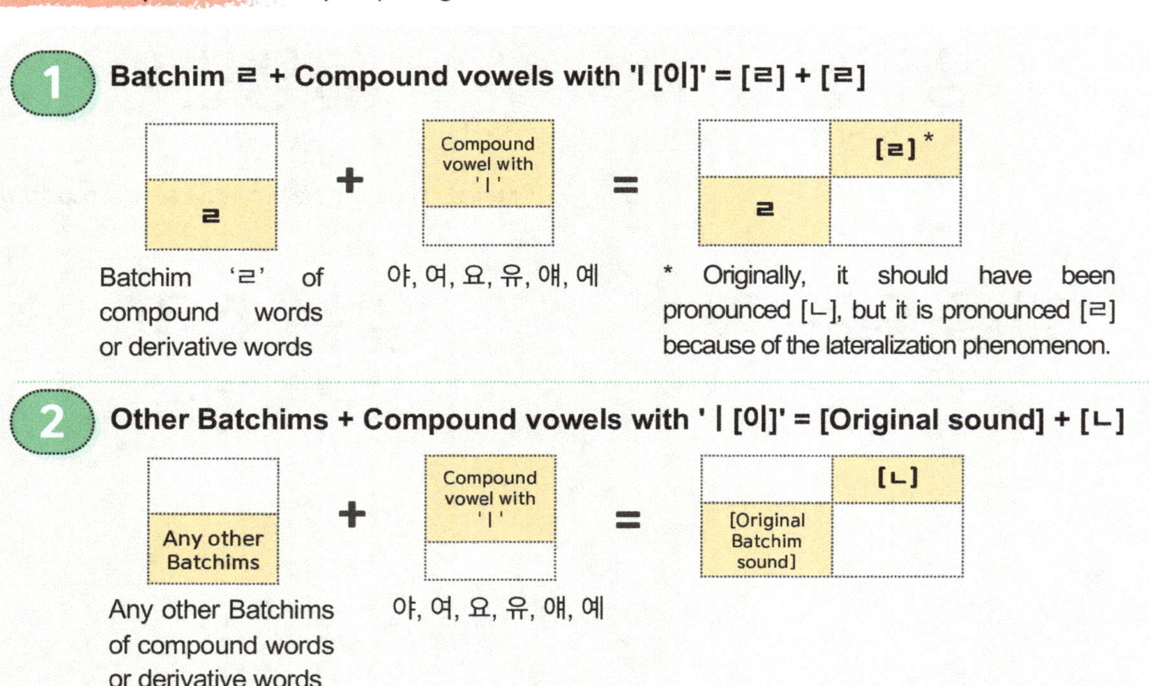

1 Batchim ㄹ + Compound vowels with 'ㅣ [이]' = [ㄹ] + [ㄹ]

Batchim '‘ㄹ’' of compound words or derivative words

야, 여, 요, 유, 얘, 예

* Originally, it should have been pronounced [ㄴ], but it is pronounced [ㄹ] because of the lateralization phenomenon.

2 Other Batchims + Compound vowels with 'ㅣ [이]' = [Original sound] + [ㄴ]

Any other Batchims of compound words or derivative words

야, 여, 요, 유, 얘, 예

This phenomenon has unique features which you need to know.

a) It is **ONLY** demonstrated in the compound or derivative words.

b) It is an **OPTIONAL** phonological phenomenon as it depends on the word or expression. Therefore, some words can be pronounced not reflecting this phenomenon. (i.e., 금융[금늉/그뮹] finance)

c) It is common to be seen with another phenomenon simultaneously.

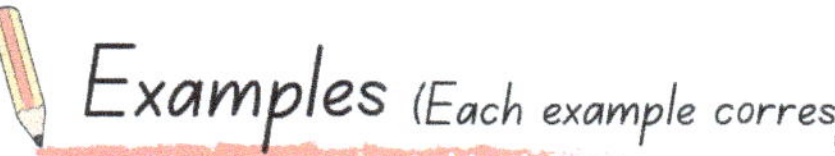 $Examples$ *(Each example corresponds to the number provided on the previous page)*

1

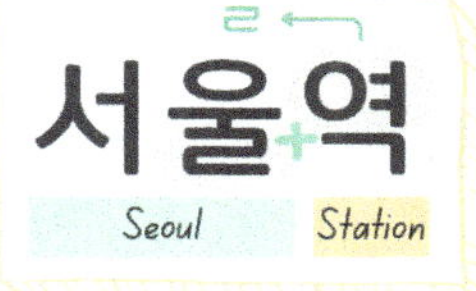

[서울력]
Seoul Station

[휘발류]
Gasoline, Petrol

2

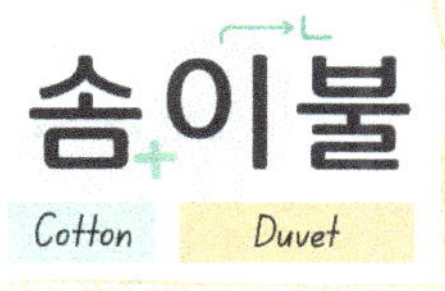

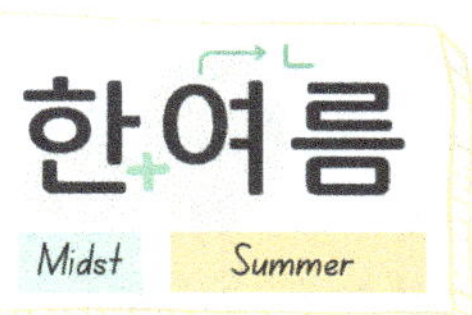

[솜니불]
Cotton comforter(duvet)

[한녀름]
Midsummer, the middle of summer

다음 단어들을 듣고 따라 읽으세요.

Listen to the words and repeat them after the narrator.

1

주말여행

[주말려행]

Weekend trip
(주말 weekend + 여행 trip)

2

알약

[알략]

Tablet, pill
(알 a small and round shaped object +약 medicine)

3

담요

[담뇨]

Blanket
(담 a piece of fur +요 bedding)

4

색연필

[생년필]

Nasalization is also shown in the syllable '색'

Colored pencil
(색 color + 연필 pencil)

5

식용유

[시굥뉴]

Cooking oil
(식용 edible + 유 oil)

6

앞일

[압닐]

Future
(앞 ahead + 일 day)

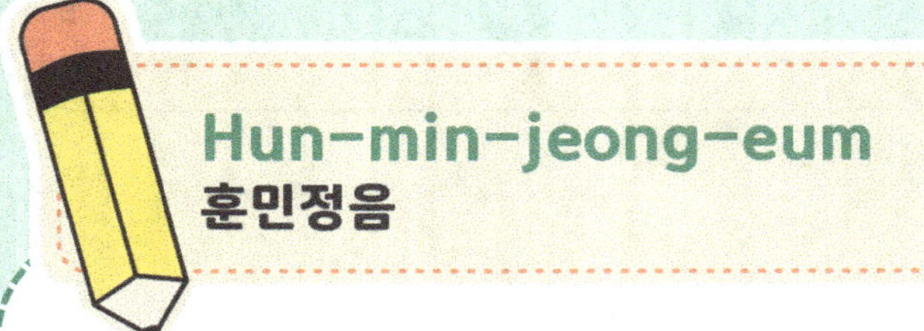

Before the creation of Hangul

Before King Sejong the Great created Hangul, traditional Chinese characters known as Hanja(한자) were used as the written language in Korea. However, writing Korean using Hanja required memorizing thousands of characters, which took ten years to learn the necessary characters and another decade to write properly. This made writing in Hanja inefficient, as the Korean language has different sounds and grammar from Chinese. As a result, many common people who could not afford a proper education were illiterate, leading to widespread illiteracy issue.

King Sejong the Great 세종대왕 (1397–1450)

Creation of 훈민정음 (Hun-min-jeong-eum) (1443)

King Sejong the Great (reign 1418-1450) recognized the need for a simpler and more accessible writing system. As a result, he created 훈민정음 (Hun-min-jeong-eum), which later became known as 한글 (Hangul), with the intention of making it easier for the common people to learn and write. To emphasize its importance, he gave it the name 훈(instruction) 민(people) 정(correct) 음(sound), meaning "the correct sounds for instructing the people." However, Hangul faced significant resistance from elites who feared that it might damage diplomatic relations with China. Additionally, modern scholars believe that elites during that time were apprehensive about spreading knowledge to the common people and worried that it might weaken their control. As a result, 훈민정음 (Hun-min-jeong-eum) was used for a long time only by common people and women and was largely disregarded by elites.

After the creation of Hangul (15-19th century)

Despite elites' opposition during the initial period of usage of Hangul, due to its efficiency in writing Korean, it became widely used by all classes, from common people to the royal family. As a result, many works of literature, novels, and newspapers were written in Hangul from the mid-Joseon period (16th-18th century). In 1894, King Gojong (reign 1864-1907) designated Hangul as the 국문 (National Script) and mandated that all legislation be written using Hangul.

Japanese colonization period (1910-1945)

During the period of Japanese occupation in Korea, the Japanese language was declared the official language, which meant that the use of spoken and written Korean was prohibited in public. To counter this, Ju Si-gyeong (주시경), a scholar and one of the leaders to print the first newspaper in Korean and English called 독립신문(Dongnip Sinmun) also brought forward the name Hangul (한글) meaning 으뜸가는 글(the Great Script), 하나밖에 없는 글(the Only One Script).

After the independence (1945~)

Although Korea has been divided into two separate governments since the Korean War of 1950-1953, both North and South Korea have continued to use Hangul as their writing system. As a result, minor spelling and vocabulary variations have emerged due to differing political ideologies. Nonetheless, Hangul remains a treasured symbol of Korean cultural identity and a source of pride and resilience for both citizens. To honor this heritage, Hangul Day is celebrated on October 9th in South Korea and January 15th in North Korea. UNESCO also recognized the cultural significance and contribution to the global linguistic diversity of Hangul by designating it as a Masterpiece of the Oral and Intangible Heritage of Humanity in 1997.

世宗御製訓民正音
나랏말ᄊᆞ미
中國에달아
文字와로서르ᄉᆞᄆᆞᆺ디아니ᄒᆞᆯᄊᆡ
이런젼ᄎᆞ로어린百姓이니르고져
홇배이셔도
ᄆᆞᄎᆞᆷ내제ᄠᅳ들시러펴디몯홇노미하
니라
내이ᄅᆞᆯ為ᄒᆞ야어엿비너겨
새로스믈여듧字ᄅᆞᆯᄆᆡᄀᆞᆯ노니
사ᄅᆞᆷ마다ᄒᆡᅇᅧ수ᄫᅵ니겨날로ᄡᅮ메便
安킈ᄒᆞ고져ᄒᆞᇙᄯᆞᄅᆞ미니라

훈민정음 언해본, 1459
(Hun-min-jeong-eum Eonhaebon, 1459)
Source: Crowdpic

This version is extensively annotated in hangul, with all hanja transcribed with small hangul to their lower right.

나라의 말이 중국과 달라 문자(한자)와는 서로 맞지 아니하여서 이런 까닭으로 어리석은(글을 모르는) 백성들이 말하고자 하는 바 있어도 마침내 제 뜻을 능히 펴지 못하는 사람이 많으니, 내 이를 위하여 (그들을) 가엾게 여겨 새롭게 스물여덟 자를 만드노니 사람마다 쉽게 익혀서 날마다 쓰는 데 편하게 하고자 할 따름이니라.

As the language spoken in this country is distinct from that of China, it does not correspond with the Chinese characters. As a result, despite their desire to communicate, many illiterate individuals struggle to express themselves effectively. Feeling disheartened by this, I commissioned the creation of 28 new letters. My hope is that these letters will be easy to learn and convenient for everyday use by all people.

 koreanstudycafe.official

koreanstudycafe.official
부산 감천 문화 마을의 예쁘고 알록달록한 집들을 잊을 수 없을 것 같다. I won't forget these pretty and colorful houses in Gamcheon Culture Village, Busan.

REPUBLIC OF KOREA
SEOUL
ADMITTED
JUL 16
SEOUL AIRPORT

4

Let's Practice Reading and Writing Korean

한국어 읽기와 쓰기를 연습해요

Daily Korean Expressions

 **Track 86**

Listen carefully to each expression, repeat it aloud, and write it in the blank boxes.

안녕하세요?
Hello. [안녕하세요]

1	안녕하세요	

안녕히 가세요.
Bye. (When the listener leaves from the place) [안녕히 가세요]

2	안녕히 가세요	

안녕히 계세요. 
Bye. (When the listener stays at the place) [안녕히 게세요/안녕히 계세요]

3	안녕히 계세요	

다음에 또 만나요.

See you next time again. [다으메 또 만나요]

4

다음에 또 만나요

만나서 반갑습니다.

Nice to meet you. [만나서 반갑씁니다]

5

만나서 반갑습니다

죄송합니다.

I'm sorry. [죄송함니다]

6

죄송합니다

괜찮아요.

It's okay. [괜차나요]

7

괜찮아요

감사합니다. 

Thank you. [감사함니다]

8

감사합니다	

# 아니에요.

In greeting conversation, it is used as "You're welcome." [아니에요]

9

아니에요	

어떻게 지냈어요? 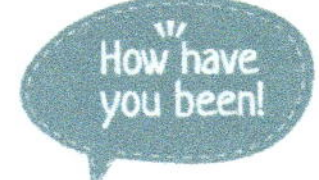

How have you been? [어떠케 지내써요]

10

어떻게 지냈어요	

# 잘 지냈어요.

I've been well. [잘 지내써요]

11

잘 지냈어요	

잘 못 지냈어요.

I haven't been well (But literally, it means "I couldn't be well") [잘 몯 지내써요]

잘 못 지냈어요

오늘 날씨가 어때요?

How's the weather today? [오늘 날씨가 어때요]

오늘 날씨가 어때요

좋아요.

It's good. [조아요]

좋아요

별로예요.

It's not very good. [별로에요/별로예요]

별로예요

좋은 하루 되세요.

Have a good day. [조은 하루 되세요]

16

좋은 하루 되세요

화이팅하세요.

Cheer up, Good luck, Break a leg, You got this. etc. [화이팅하세요]

17

화이팅하세요

다 잘 될 거예요.

Everything will be okay. [다 잘 될 꺼에요/꺼예요]

18

다 잘 될 거예요

걱정하지 마세요.

Don't worry (about it). [걱쩡하지 마세요]

19

걱정하지 마세요

맛있게 드세요. 

20

Enjoy your meal. [마싣께/마딛께 드세요]

맛있게 드세요

 # 잘 먹겠습니다.

21

Thank you for the food. (But literally, it means "I will eat well") [잘 먹께씀니다]

잘 먹겠습니다

생일 축하합니다. 

22

Happy birthday. [생일 추카함니다]

생일 축하합니다

 # 새해 복 많이 받으세요.

23

Happy new year. [새해 복 마니 바드세요]

새해 복 많이 받으세요

www.ingramcontent.com/pod-product-compliance
Lightning Source LLC
Chambersburg PA
CBHW081026060726
47593CB00020B/2908